P9-CQK-838

UGARIT

CITIES OF THE BIBLICAL WORLD

General Editor:
Graham I. Davies, Lecturer in Divinity,
Cambridge University

Other Titles:
Excavation in Palestine, Roger Moorey, Senior Assistant Keeper,
 Department of Antiquities, Ashmolean Museum, Oxford
Qumran, Philip R. Davies, Lecturer in Biblical Studies, University of
 Sheffield
Jericho, John R. Bartlett, Lecturer in Divinity and Fellow of Trinity
 College, Dublin

In Preparation:
Megiddo, Graham I. Davies

CITIES OF THE BIBLICAL WORLD

Ugarit

(Ras Shamra)

Adrian Curtis

Lecturer in Old Testament Studies,
University of Manchester

William B. Eerdmans Publishing Company
Grand Rapids, Michigan

First published in 1985

Copyright © Adrian H. W. Curtis 1985

First American edition published 1985 through special arrangement with Lutterworth
by Wm. B. Eerdmans Publishing Co., 255 Jefferson S.E., Grand Rapids, MI 49503

All rights reserved. No part of this publication may be reproduced, stored in a
retrieval system, or transmitted in any form or by any means, electronic, mechanical,
photocopying, recording or otherwise, without the prior permission of
Lutterworth Press, 7 All Saints' Passage, Cambridge, CB2 3LS.

ISBN 0–8028–0166–8

Printed in Great Britain

To Hilary, Daniel and Jonathan

72530

Contents

List of Illustrations

Preface

The Canaanites and their religion, and in particular the God Baal, are roundly denounced in the Old Testament. The graphic description of Elijah's great contest with the prophets of Baal on Mount Carmel is one of the most familiar of Old Testament stories, while the poignant pleading of Hosea that his fellow Israelites should turn from the 'adultery' of Baal worship to their 'true love', Yahweh, provides one of the high points in the prophetic teaching. It was a chance discovery in 1928 that was to lead to the excavation by archaeologists of the site of Ras Shamra in Syria (the ancient city of Ugarit) and the unearthing of the Ugaritic literature. This, in turn, has provided a more direct witness to the beliefs and practices of the Canaanites, despite the many problems of interpretation of both the written and artefactual material, and has enabled students of the Bible not merely to take a less jaundiced view of the Canaanites but to appreciate something of their culture and religion, and its importance for understanding certain Old Testament passages.

This book attempts to introduce the reader to Ugarit and its literature. It provides a brief description of the discovery of the site and the early stages of its excavation and of the decipherment of the Ugaritic language. The city's history is outlined and aspects of its life and culture are considered. It has been felt more appropriate to place the summary of some of the important Ugaritic myths and legends (Chapter 4) before the discussion of the religion of Ugarit (Chapter 5). Finally there is a consideration of some of the ways in which the Ugaritic material may be of relevance to the study of the Bible.

Dates given in the book normally follow the scheme adopted in R. de Vaux, *The Early History of Israel* (2 volumes, London, 1978). Uncertainty about the vocalisation of Ugaritic creates difficulties over the 'correct' spelling of proper names, and in a number of instances I have been content to use what have become traditional spellings, e.g. Baal, Keret.

The bulk of the original manuscript was completed in 1981, with some amendments in 1982; a number of works have become available to me in the interim of which I should have wished to take note, including some which should be added to the suggestions for further reading. Particular mention should be made of: A. Caquot and M. Sznycer, *Ugaritic Religion* (Iconography of Religions XV, 8), Leiden, 1980; P. C. Craigie, *Ugarit and the Old Testament*, Grand Rapids, 1983; J. Day, *God's Conflict with the Dragon and the Sea*, Cambridge, 1985.

Acknowledgements

My interest in the literature from ancient Ugarit stems from my time as a post-graduate student in the Department of Biblical Criticism and Exegesis, Manchester University, when my research topic was the relevance of Ugaritic for the Psalter, with special reference to divine names, epithets and attributes. I am grateful to the Lutterworth Press for this opportunity to attempt to make more widely known something of this literature and the context from which it emerged. I am also glad to be able to acknowledge the assistance and encouragement over the years of my former supervisor and present colleague, the Rev. A. A. Anderson.

In connection with the preparation of this volume, I must express my gratitude to Dr G. I. Davies, the general editor of the series, for his comments and suggestions which removed many blemishes from the original manuscript; to Dr J. Healey, Mr A. Millard, and Mr P. Parr for their kind willingness to allow me to reproduce their photographs of the site; and to Mrs Frances Shaw, Miss Eileen Thompson and Mr David Game of Lutterworth Press for their help and patience.

Those familiar with the literature on Ugarit will realise my indebtedness to many writers on the subject. In particular the sections on the history of Ugarit owe much to M. S. Drower's survey in the third edition of the *Cambridge Ancient History*, and the passages on the city and its major buildings to G. Saadé's descriptions of the site. In a book in which references have been kept to a minimum, it is appropriate that my debt to these and many other writers be expressed at the outset.

Abbreviations

CTA	*Corpus des Tablettes en Cunéiformes Alphabétiques Découvertes à Ras Shamra-Ugarit de 1929 à 1939*, Mlle A. Herdner
JSS	*Journal of Semitic Studies*
JTS	*Journal of Theological Studies*
MRS	*Mission de Ras Shamra*
MT	Masoretic Text
PRU	*Le Palais royal d'Ugarit*
UF	*Ugarit-Forschungen*
VT	*Vetus Testamentum*
ZDPV	*Zeitschrift des Deutschen Palästina-Vereins*

Chronological Table

	UGARIT	EGYPT	MESOPOTAMIA AND ANATOLIA	PALESTINE
2000	MIDDLE BRONZE I	*Middle Kingdom* XII DYNASTY		
1950	? Temple of Baal	(Sesostris I)		
1900	MIDDLE BRONZE II	(Sesostris II)		
1850	? Niqmaddu I Yaqarum I	(Amenemhet III)		
1800		XIII & XIV DYNASTY		
1750	MIDDLE BRONZE III ? Hurrians seize control	*Second Intermediate Period* The Hyksos	(Hammurabi of Babylon)	
1700	New quarter built ? Puruqqu	XV–XVII DYNASTY		? PATRIARCHAL PERIOD
1650				
1600	Northern Palace and sanctuary LATE BRONZE I			
1550		*New Kingdom* XVIII DYNASTY (Amosis)	Kingdom of Mitanni	
1500		(Tuthmosis I) (Tuthmosis II)		
1450	LATE BRONZE II	(Tuthmosis III)	Late Hittite Empire Egypto-Mitannian alliance	
1400	Beginning of 'Golden Age'. Royal Palace begun in 15th. cent. Ammistamru I LATE BRONZE III	(Amenophis II) (Tuthmosis IV) (Amenophis III) (Amenophis IV/ Akhenaten)		Amarna letters

16

	UGARIT	EGYPT	MESOPOTAMIA AND ANATOLIA	PALESTINE
1350	Niqmaddu II Arḫalbu		(Shuppiluliumash I)	
1300	Niqmepa	XIX DYNASTY (Ramesses II)	(Muwatallish) Battle of Qadesh	Exodus
1250	? Aḫat-milki Ammistamru II Ibiranu Niqmaddu III 'Ammurapi			
1200	Destruction of Ugarit	XX DYNASTY Defeat of Sea Peoples		Settlement of Israelite tribes
1150				

Chronological Table of the Second Millennium BC.
(Only the names of persons mentioned in the text are included)

Introduction

On the coast of Syria, some seven miles north of modern Latakia (ancient *Laodicea ad mare*) and about twenty-five miles south of the mouth of the river Orontes, at a point whence the island of Cyprus can be seen on a clear day, is the bay of Minet el-Beida ('White Harbour'). The whiteness of the rocks at the entrance to the harbour had also led the Greeks to name it White Harbour (*Leukos Limēn*). It was the chance find of a cemetery close to the harbour just over half a century ago which sparked off a chain of events leading to an archaeological excavation whose results have made a considerable impact on ancient Near Eastern and biblical studies, thanks in particular to the discovery of a hitherto unknown Semitic language.

In the spring of 1928, a Syrian farmer from Bourj al-Qaṣab, named Mahmoud Mella Az-Zîr, was ploughing a plot of land near the harbour. His work was halted when his plough struck a stone slab. He had previously come across antiquities in the field, so later that same day he returned with some companions. They removed a thin covering of soil and uncovered several stone slabs which, when raised, revealed a tomb vault containing a number of small pottery items. The discovery was reported to the governor of the local territory, and then to the *Service des Antiquités en Syrie et au Liban*; at the direction of Charles Virolleaud, Léon Albanèse went to examine the site, and identified it as a royal necropolis. Some pieces of pottery were discovered which were identified with Cypriot and Mycenean ceramics of about the thirteenth century BC, but the site did not appear on first examination to be particularly promising. Samples of the pottery and the plan of the funeral vault were sent to the Louvre where they came to the attention of René Dussaud, Keeper of the Department of Oriental Antiquities. Dussaud noted the similarity between the tomb vault and ancient Cretan tombs, and suggested that an important city might have been situated nearby, of which this was the cemetery. Thus, attention was soon to turn to the nearby hill known as Ras Shamra ('fennel headland') because of the plants which grew there in profusion, and which, as Albanèse had already pointed out, had all the appearance of being a *tell*, i.e. an artificial mound caused by successive occupations and destructions of cities on the site.

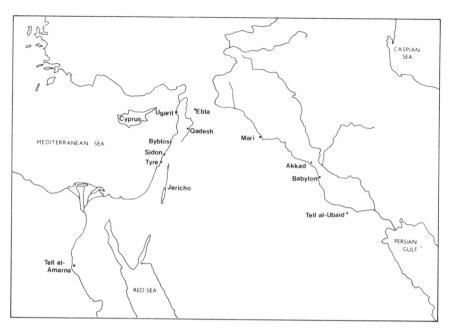

Figure 1   The Ancient Near East

Excavations were carried out under the sponsorship of the *Académie des Inscriptions et Belles Lettres* of Paris, under the direction of C.F.A. Schaeffer.

The first excavation team arrived on the site just before Easter 1929, with a detachment of soldiers for protection, and a camp was established. The equipment had been carried by camel, since the roads in the locality were unsuitable for motor vehicles. The immediate vicinity was surveyed, and traces of occupation from the Neolithic to the Roman period were found within a relatively small radius. On 2nd April the excavation commenced in earnest, and within three days it was established that a necropolis had been discovered. This turned out to comprise two very different areas; the seaward section contained mainly pottery and animal bones with no trace of human remains, while the other contained vaulted tombs. Artefacts discovered in the area of the necropolis soon began to reveal the cosmopolitan nature of the city. Among a varied group of objects, which included bronze statuettes decorated with gold or silver, and a strange clay object in the shape of a ladle, was a bronze hawk wearing the double crown of Upper and Lower Egypt. Near this was a large, rather roughly made, two-handled vase broken by a stone, and a Cypriot bowl. Once these had been removed, another

19

Plate 1 Bronze statuette of a hawk wearing the crown of Egypt; probably a representation of the god Horus

hawk figure was revealed, smaller than the former, but encrusted with gold and holding the uraeus (a serpent or cobra, worn by Egyptian pharaohs on their head-dresses) between its feet. A statuette of a seated figure, probably a god, with eyes encrusted with white enamel and silver, was found nearby. A little further away what was perhaps the most important of these early finds came to light. This was a statuette of a god, 22 cm high, with one leg before the other as though marching, the right hand raised above the head, the left hand held forward as though it had originally been holding something; the figure wore a tall helmet, and head and helmet were covered with gold leaf; on the chest was a silver breastplate, and the limbs bore silver armbands and greaves. On analogy with other representations already known, the figure was at first identified with the god Resheph; however, it has subsequently been thought more likely that the figure represents Baal.

20

Plate 2   Statuette originally thought to represent Resheph, but probably depicting
Baal

21

Close to the statuette was a pendant of gold leaf embossed with the figure of a naked goddess holding what appeared to be a lotus in each hand, and wearing a head-dress. This was thought to be a representation of Athtarat.

The nature of the tombs themselves was of considerable interest. An unfinished tomb found in the southern section of the necropolis was of the same type, though larger, than that which had been first discovered. Next to the tomb were shafts with hive-shaped vaulted entrances, the opening covered with a large pierced stone slab upon which the neck of a large jar had been placed. Nearby were a number of images, apparently unfinished, painted red and in the shape of bulls' heads and standing females; similar figures had been found at Tiryns and Mycenae. Another feature of this locality was a type of waterfall, taking water down into the earth. Particular mention should be made of one other tomb. This was a specially constructed vaulted chamber, approached by a staircase of six steps, near the door of which was found the skull of a person aged between twenty and thirty. A hole in the vault, and the presence within the tomb of soil which had fallen through it, revealed the activity of tomb-plunderers in antiquity. No sarcophagus was found, but the jumbled bones of at least three skeletons lay on the floor, along with a number of bowls and vases. However, in their haste the tomb-robbers had failed to search the corners of the chamber, where one of the most notable and beautiful discoveries was made – an oval ivory box, whose cover bore the carving of a seated female figure (see plate 3). The style was clearly Mycenean. She was naked to the waist, but wore a full skirt; the hands were raised, and held what appeared to be ears of corn; on either side of the figure were goats standing on their hind legs. The figure is usually thought to represent a fertility goddess, and the presence of the animals suggests the *potnia thērōn* ('queen/mistress of wild animals').

On 9th May work on the site of the necropolis was halted, in order that attention could turn to the nearby mound to discover whether it concealed the ruins of the city of which the cemetery had begun to come to light. The *tell* was just over a kilometre from the necropolis, trapezoid in shape with a maximum diameter of over half a kilometre, and rose between seventeen and twenty metres above the surrounding countryside. The summit of the mound was very uneven, and bore no evidence of ancient buildings. After an examination of the mound's surface, it was decided to commence excavations at the point closest to the sea. Schaeffer suggested that the royal palace might have been located in this area because local inhabitants had reported the discovery of gold objects and cylinders in an olive orchard which was situated immediately below that part of the mound, and he thought it possible that these objects had been washed down from the *tell* by the winter rains. The choice was inspired, for almost as soon as excavations

22

Plate 3 Ivory box-lid from Minet el-Beida, thought to depict a goddess of fertility

began, there were brought to light the foundations of a large building which had been destroyed by fire. The discovery of a bronze dagger which had been distorted by the heat of the fire, and a bronze nail embedded between the blocks of a pillar enabled the building to be dated to the second millennium BC. As more of the walls, constructed of large, well-fitted blocks, began to be revealed, it became possible to produce a plan of part of the building, which had all the appearance of an important edifice. A further pointer towards the date was provided by the fragments of a granite Egyptian statue bearing hieroglyphs which were dated to the New Kingdom period (sixteenth to eleventh centuries). In order that the extent of the building might be ascertained, a second trench was begun twenty metres to the east. There foundations were discovered of the same depth and lying in the same

Plate 4   Bronze tripod, with pendants of pomegranate flowers

direction as those of the first trench; however, they appeared to belong to smaller rooms, some of which were paved. Since it seemed likely that these were storerooms it was decided to concentrate on this area.

On 14th May, in a corner of one of the rooms, was found a large tablet of baked clay, inscribed with cuneiform characters. Others soon began to emerge, lying in small groups in an area about two metres square. The effect of the conflagration which had destroyed the building had been to make the clay tablets very crumbly, so the utmost care had to be taken to preserve them. Indeed, some were removed encased in blocks of earth. They were slowly dried in the shade of a tent until they regained enough solidity to allow them to be moved. There were twenty tablets in all, the smallest measuring three centimetres by four, the largest sixteen by twenty-five, and the majority were in a hitherto unknown language. The tablets were submitted to Charles Virolleaud. Two days later, in a newly begun trench, under a paving stone, was found a deposit of arms, tools, and other articles of bronze – seventy-four items in all – all in a remarkable state of preservation. They included a tripod with pendants of pomegranate flowers, and five tools which bore cuneiform inscriptions in the same characters as those on the tablets which had so recently been discovered (see plate 5). Writing in the journal *Syria* for 1929 (in which Schaeffer gave an account of the first season's work at Ras Shamra) Virolleaud gave a preliminary description of the new language, and suggested the likelihood that the inscriptions on the tools might provide the clue to decipherment.

Plate 5   Tools inscribed, *rb khnm* (chief of the priests)

The occasional pieces of pottery found in the building were identical with that of the necropolis, dating from the end of the thirteenth century or the beginning of the twelfth. It thus appeared that the necropolis had ceased to be used when the city was destroyed.

The first season's activity on the site has been described in some detail, but subsequent campaigns must be summarised more briefly. It was a tablet discovered in 1931 which provided the confirmation of the ancient identity of the city. Towards the end of the preliminary report of the 1931 excavations (published in 1932 in *Syria*), Schaeffer reported that the tablet contained the phrase *nqmd mlk égrt* (sic), and that Virolleaud had confirmed that the last word had appeared on several tablets found in 1929. The phrase ('Niqmaddu, king of Ugarit') supported the conclusion that Ras Shamra was the site of the ancient city of Ugarit, known notably from references to such a city in the Tell el-Amarna letters. A footnote in *Syria* for 1932 mentioned that the American scholar W.F. Albright had suggested this identification in the journal *Archiv für Orientforschung* VII. It is noteworthy that J.A. Knudtzon, in his commentary on the Amarna letters (*Die El-Amarna-Tafeln*, vol. II, Leipzig, 1915, p.1016) had suggested that Ugarit must have been a harbour on the caravan routes in the north of Syria.

A total of eleven campaigns preceded the outbreak of the Second World War, and until 1935 excavations continued in the region of Minet el-Beida as well as on the *tell*. On the mound itself, excavations revealed notably the Temple of Baal, the Temple of Dagan, and the house of the high-priest which included a library containing numerous texts. Although the main concentration was given to the topmost of the main strata, some deeper trenches were dug so that the lower strata could be examined. Five principal levels were originally identified,

Level I – *c*. 1200–1600
Level II – *c*. 1600–2100
Level III – *c*. 2100–3500
Level IV – *c*. 3500–4000
Level V – Neolithic period (fifth and sixth millennia BC)

It was subsequently realised that the stratigraphy was considerably more complex, involving perhaps three or four times as many levels between the Neolithic and the Roman period (see page 41).

Excavations were interrupted by the war, but a limited resumption of the work was made in 1948; it was not until 1950 that work could go ahead in earnest. In the early campaigns after the resumption, particular attention was paid to the Royal Palace, and six collections of texts were found – the Central Archives, the Eastern Archives, the Western Archives, the Southern

Plate 6   Main entrance of the Royal Palace

Archives, the South-Western Archives, and some texts discovered actually within a firing kiln. Among the 'landmarks' of subsequent campaigns, particularly noteworthy are the following: in 1954 and 1955 excavations were extended to include the small Southern Palace; in 1956, in the course of excavations in a residential quarter, the Archives of Rap'anu came to light; in 1968 work began on the Northern Palace; the so-called House of Alabasters was discovered in 1973.

In the course of the brief survey of excavations, we have noted that a number of groups of texts were discovered – the Library of the High Priest, the Palace Archives, and the Archives of Rap'anu. In addition, we should note the discovery of archives within the small Southern Palace, a private library found in a home in the residential area at the south of the *tell*, and the library of someone, perhaps a priest, who practised divination, found at the southern edge of the necropolis. A feature of the texts is the surprising variety of languages represented; in addition to numerous texts in Akkadian, other languages were Sumerian, Hittite, Egyptian, Hurrian, the Minoan script of Cyprus, and a hitherto unknown language. The large number of tablets in this unknown language gave rise to the belief that this must be the

27

local language, spoken by the majority of the inhabitants of the city. Thus the language has come to be known as Ugaritic.

The Ugaritic scribes had borrowed their method of writing from their Mesopotamian neighbours; cuneiform signs were produced by means of a stylus on soft clay which was subsequently baked hard. However, the major difference between this writing system and those of Mesopotamia was that it employed only thirty signs (one of which was employed only in the transliteration of Hurrian) (see figure 2). It therefore appeared to be an alphabetic rather than a syllabic or ideographic script – a description which should perhaps be modified slightly by noting that Ugaritic employs three different signs to represent the consonant equivalent to Hebrew *aleph*, depending on whether it is associated with the vowel *a*, *i*, or *u*. Nevertheless, the discovery of 'alphabet' tablets listing the consonants in the same order as they appear in the Hebrew alphabet (with the extra signs inserted at appropriate points) means that there may still be some justification in seeing in Ugaritic the earliest known alphabet. It is difficult to be certain how the script originated; it is possible that it was adapted from the more complicated Akkadian script, or that it was a modification of a linear script already known in the region to facilitate its writing on soft clay tablets.

A remarkable feature of the story of the discoveries at Ugarit is the speed with which the new language was deciphered. The first texts were published with great alacrity by Virolleaud, allowing other scholars to work on them, while he continued to do so himself. H. Bauer of the University of Halle, and E. Dhorme of the *Ecole Biblique* in Jerusalem, working independently, identified a number of signs and several words. (It is noteworthy that both Dhorme and Bauer had had experience in the cracking of codes and ciphers). The combined results of the work of these three scholars was that the significance of almost all the signs, and the identification of a number of words, had been achieved within a matter of months.

The decipherment depended on a mixture of inspired guesses and great expertise in languages and in ciphers. The relatively small number of signs led to the surmise that the script was alphabetic. The presence of a small vertical wedge between groups of signs was taken to be a word-divider; this suggested that the words were short, and supported the assumption that the language was Semitic. We mentioned earlier that Virolleaud had suggested that the inscriptions on the bronze tools might provide the clue to decipherment. Six signs on one of the tools were taken to be the name of the owner or maker; in fact the signs turned out to represent *rb khnm*, 'the chief of the priests', identifying the owner of the building where the weapons and other bronze articles had been discovered. At the beginning of one of the tablets, the same six signs were found, preceded by a sign composed of three

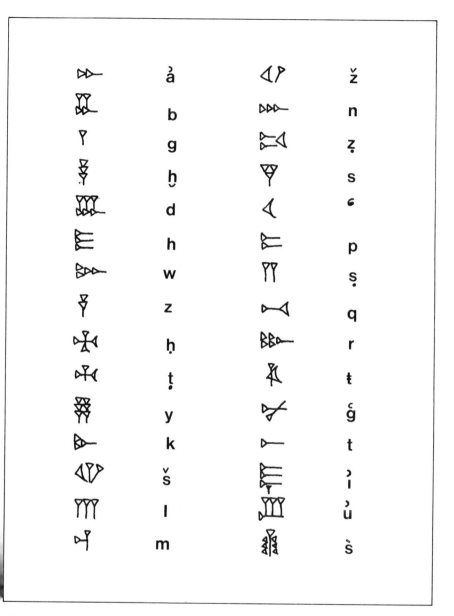

Figure 2   The Ugaritic Script. The signs are given in the order in which they appear in Ugaritic alphabet tablets.

vertical wedges. On the assumption that the tablet was a communication addressed *to* the person whose name was thought to follow, the value *l*, commonly used to indicate the preposition 'to', was assigned to this symbol. Virolleaud then began to look for other words containing this letter, and to match them with possible equivalents in other Semitic languages, especially common words or titles. A three letter group with the proposed *l* in the middle suggested the word *mlk*, 'king', and this was supported by the discovery of a similar four-letter group wherein the first letter was repeated at the end, and which could be read as *mlkm* ('kings'). Other words containing the letter *l* were soon discovered – the name of the god Baal, and the numerals three and thirty; then a tablet containing a column of numbers enabled several more signs to be identified.

Bauer's approach had been to calculate the frequency of various signs, and to note their position; he also listed various prefixes and suffixes, and monosyllabic words which might be represented by a single consonant, and which might be expected to appear in what was presumed to be a West Semitic language. Like Virolleaud, he had soon identified *l*, and, noting the recurrence of a pair of letters in what was thought to be a list of names, he suggested that they might represent *bn*, 'son'. In 1930 he published a list of twenty-seven signs and suggested identifications for twenty-five of them, many of which proved to be correct (*Entzifferung der Keilschrifttafeln von Ras Schamra*, Halle/Saale, 1930). Dhorme, too, had looked for words containing *l*, and had identified the name of the god Baal. However, having obtained the consonant *b* he noted two two-letter words beginning with *b*, which he thought to be *bn*, 'son', and *bt*, 'daughter' or 'house'. Unfortunately he got them the wrong way round, and so confused *n* with *t* and vice versa. Once Dhorme had seen Bauer's preliminary decipherment, and realised his mistake, he was able to make rapid progress ('Un nouvel alphabet Sémitique', *Revue Biblique* XXXIX, 1930, pp.571 ff). In 1931, just a year after the first publication of texts, Virolleaud published his translation of what he called the Epic of Aleyan and Mot (*àliyn* is now seen to be an epithet of Baal, meaning 'the Victor').

It is important to note that, although the new language has come to be known as Ugaritic, the script has been discovered in other places. Some of these discoveries have been made fairly close to Ugarit, at Ibn Hani, Tell Sukas, and at Tell Nebi-Mend (ancient Qadesh on the Orontes). Two sites in Lebanon have revealed inscriptions – a jar-handle from Kâmed el-Lôz, and the neck of a jar from Sarafend. From Israel, we note inscriptions on tablets from Beth Shemesh and from Ta'anach, and on a dagger discovered near Mount Tabor. Also noteworthy is the fact that, at Ugarit itself, the script was used for the writing of the Hurrian language.

The inscribed tablets were found to contain a very varied literature. The fact that many languages were employed in the city must have caused a problem for the scribes of Ugarit. It was not sufficient to be familiar with the local language and with Akkadian, the lingua franca of the time; thus it was necessary for 'dictionaries' to be produced listing, for example, words in Akkadian with their equivalents in Sumerian or Hurrian. Numerous inventories and lists of people, places etc., have been discovered. The archives contained diplomatic, military, legal, administrative and commercial texts. Other discoveries included private letters and even a prescription for the treatment of ailing horses. In addition to the secular material, there was a large corpus of religious texts which included lists of sacrifices and of deities, ritual texts, and the longer poems which recounted the activities of the gods.

These last were seized upon by Old Testament scholars, for while much of the Ugaritic material was of considerable linguistic value in its help with the elucidation of aspects of the Hebrew text of the Old Testament, here at last was a direct witness to the religion of Canaan, whose writing could be dated to the period *c*. 1400–1350 BC. Previously our knowledge of Canaanite religion came mainly from the Old Testament itself, where it was roundly condemned, especially by the prophets. Other information was also derived from Eusebius of Caesarea who included in his *Preparation for the Gospel* certain fragments, translated into Greek by Philo of Byblos, of a *Phoenician History* reputed to have been written 'before the Trojan times' by the learned Sanchuniathon of Beirut. But with the availability of the Ugaritic literature, students of the Old Testament gained a much more direct witness, despite the many problems, to the religious thought of the ancient Canaanites amongst whom the Israelites settled. Here was a literature more closely related to that of the Hebrews in terms of location, time, and linguistic affinity, than the Mesopotamian and Egyptian literatures which had been available to scholars for many years.

Although the date of the texts means that they provide a direct witness to Canaanite life and beliefs as they were prior to the establishment of the Hebrew tribes in Palestine, we are doubtless closer to an understanding of Canaanite religion as it continued to be after the settlement, when considerable tension must have existed with Yahwism, and when syncretistic tendencies were common. It is not to be wondered at that the Israelites, who adopted much of the material culture of the Canaanites, would adopt cultic practices and religious ideas from their neighbours. It has even been argued that the Old Testament should be seen as a phase in the development of Canaanite literature. Certainly it began to be claimed that the study of Ugaritic was vital to Old Testament scholarship. Indeed, some of the claims made for the Ugaritic material were grandiose in the extreme, bordering on a 'pan-Ugariticism' reminiscent of the 'pan-Babylonianism' of an earlier generation. On the whole, a more sober appreciation of the relevance of the Ugaritic material has prevailed. Attention is paid to the differences between Ugaritic and Hebrew ideas as well as to the similarities, and the fact that borrowing from another culture frequently involves adaptation. Furthermore, although it is true that Ugarit is geographically closer to Israel than the other great cultural centres of the ancient Near East, it is nevertheless a considerable distance away. Indeed, the question has been asked whether Ugarit should really be classed as a 'Canaanite' city, since it lies outside the boundaries of Canaan as defined in the Old Testament (cf. especially Numbers 34:2–12). The fact that Ugarit was destroyed before the establishment of Israel makes it virtually certain that there was no *direct* influence of the former upon the latter. However, that the Ugaritic material is of great relevance to the study of the Old Testament cannot be seriously questioned.

Notes on Further Reading

Official Publications
The official publications of the discoveries at Ras Shamra/Ugarit are to be found in the series of volumes *Mission de Ras Shamra (MRS)*, published under the direction of C.F.A. Schaeffer in Paris since 1936. The series incorporates the various volumes entitled *Ugaritica* and *Le Palais royal d'Ugarit (PRU)*.

Periodicals
The earliest publication of the excavations at Minet el-Beida and Ras Shamra, and the primary editions of many of the texts appeared in the journal *Syria*. Articles on the discoveries at Ugarit and their significance have appeared and continue to appear in various learned journals which deal with the ancient Near East, the Semitic languages, and biblical studies. Particular mention should be made of the annual publication *Ugarit-Forschungen (UF)*, and the *Newsletter for Ugaritic Studies* edited by P.C. Craigie.

Bibliography
A useful select bibliography of Ugarit and its texts can be found in J.C.L. Gibson, *Canaanite Myths and Legends*, Edinburgh, 1978. For a detailed bibliography the reader should consult M. Dietrich, O. Loretz, P-R. Berger and J. Sanmartín, *Ugarit Bibliographie 1928–1966*, 4 vols., Neukirchen-Vluyn, 1973.

The Ugaritic Language

The standard textbook on the Ugaritic language is C.H. Gordon, *Ugaritic Textbook*, Rome, 1965 with supplement 1967; this work contains a Ugaritic glossary, as does J.C.L. Gibson, *Canaanite Myths and Legends*, mentioned above; cf. also J. Aistleitner, *Wörterbuch der ugaritischen Sprache*, Berlin, 1963; R.E. Whitaker, *A Concordance of the Ugaritic Literature*, Cambridge Massachusetts, 1972.

1

The Early History of Ugarit

Habitation began in the vicinity of Ras Shamra many centuries before the earliest signs of occupation of the *tell*, since traces of the Palaeolithic culture have been found some seven kilometres to the north. Nevertheless, Ras Shamra itself is a site of great antiquity. At the bottom of the soundings made to establish how far back the history of the site could be traced, at a depth of about eighteen metres, was found evidence of occupation in the Neolithic period, i.e. before the fifth millennium BC. These earliest inhabitants used tools of ivory, bone and flint, though no pottery was found in the very lowest stratum, perhaps because they used simple vessels made of perishable materials or of improperly baked clay which would be virtually impossible to distinguish from the surrounding soil. In the layers immediately above, at a depth of sixteen or seventeen metres, was found a relatively advanced type of pottery, in addition to vessels made of stone. The pottery was not yet painted, but was sometimes decorated with spots or small marks made with some sharp object before baking.

The origins of this earliest population are obscure, but resemblances between the pottery found in level V at Ras Shamra and that discovered elsewhere suggest that the population of Syria and the region of the upper Euphrates had some common characteristics. Indeed, analogies have been noted between the Neolithic pottery of Ras Shamra and Jericho, suggesting the possibility of contacts with Palestine.

Excavations of level IV have been somewhat restricted, and no remains of metal objects have yet been discovered, although at the time represented by this level the use of copper was becoming widespread elsewhere. Tools of flint, obsidian (a volcanic rock) and bone were used. However, the occupants of the site belonged to a considerably more advanced civilisation as is evidenced by the remarkably fine pottery. Much of the ceramic ware was not only made of a much finer material, but was now richly decorated with painting, sometimes in a number of colours. From this level come the remains of dwellings comprising rectangular rooms; evidence of round hearths and circular structures – perhaps silos – has also been found.

During the fourth and early third millennia BC, Ras Shamra must have had some contacts with Mesopotamia, since level III has revealed a painted pottery of a type known from the upper layers of al Ubaid. The pottery was polychrome, decorated with geometrical designs painted in browns, dark blues, and blacks, on a grey or buff-coloured background. The Early Bronze Age (c. 3000–2100) saw a rapid advance in metal-working throughout the ancient Near East, and bronze weapons and tools from this period have been unearthed at Ras Shamra. This was a time of population movements from Mesopotamia and the upper Euphrates, and although it is not clear what, if any, were the centres of the culture which spread so far and wide, it does seem that Ras Shamra came much more clearly under Mesopotamian influence. This spread of Mesopotamian culture may have helped to pave the way for the territorial expansions of Sargon the Great, king of Akkad and his grandson Naram-Sin, in the latter part of the third millennium. Indeed, Sargon claims to have traversed this region, and it is not impossible that he passed through Ras Shamra. It was on the Mediterranean coast that the kings of Akkad sought outlets for the products of Mesopotamia in exchange for materials which they lacked, such as wood and stone for building. Thus Ras Shamra and its port probably formed one of the important staging points between Mesopotamia and the Mediterranean world.

The end of the Akkadian Empire, brought about by the incursion of the Guti from the Zagros Mountains in about 2200 BC was the signal for a period of turmoil and disorder in the ancient Near East. Population migrations disrupted the political stability of the area, and, for Syria, this was a period of economic distress. That this was a dark age in the history of Ras Shamra is suggested by the upper layers of level III, reflecting the late third millennium. The remains suggest an impoverished, unsophisticated civilisation, and that the quality of the pottery had lost much of its refinement, being more reminiscent of that of the prehistoric layers. It is possible that a destruction and conflagration of the city which seems to have taken place in the latter part of the third millennium and which removed a proportion of the city's inhabitants, is to be linked with this period of crisis.

In fact, this was a turning point in the history of the city. As already indicated, this was a time of population migration, and important displacements of people were affecting the region of Syria. The Amorites were involved in a great expansion movement, and with them came groups variously referred to as Proto-Phoenicians, Phoenicians, or Canaanites. As these peoples moved northwards along the Mediterranean coast they began to settle down. These new inhabitants, with a remarkable instinct for commerce, must have realised the tremendous commercial potential of this ideally situated harbour. Henceforth the importance of the city was to lie in its situation at the crossroads between the Asian and Mediterranean worlds.

No longer was Ras Shamra merely the western outpost of Mesopotamian influence and departure point for Mesopotamian merchandise. Rather, ships brought *to* Ras Shamra the produce of the Mediterranean world, and, from further afield, from the Red Sea, products such as gold, fragrant perfumes and incense, in exchange for wood, and copper, bronze and, rarely, iron tools and weapons. There was also commerce in horses. Remains dating from this period suggest that architecture was characterised by the use of large building blocks. Traces of a rampart have been discovered, as have bronze weapons, and a kiln made of clay and small stones which contained two pots of Canaanite type. Also from this period was found a workshop for the manufacture of olive oil; presses and vats were discovered *in situ*, along with a large stone mallet for crushing fruit, and even olive stones.

The importance of Ras Shamra, and its economic activity increased in the early second millennium. First the Pharaohs of the eleventh and twelfth dynasties in Egypt, and later king Hammurabi the Great in Babylon, re-established the prestige of the two great powers, and the Fertile Crescent was in a state of peace. The city, lying as it did at the point of contact between the two empires, was able to prosper. In this period sanctuaries were erected by the inhabitants in honour of various deities. The temple which appeared to be the most ancient was that dedicated to Dagan, a Semitic deity whose cult spread with the advance of the Amorites. Another important sanctuary was consecrated to Baal/Hadad, who appears, from the number of representations discovered, to have enjoyed great popularity and prestige. But more detailed discussion of these and other deities must wait until a later chapter.

It was probably from the beginning of the second millennium at least that the city was known as Ugarit. Indeed, the discovery of the name *u-ga-ra-tim* in the archives from Ebla may be a reference to Ugarit and may suggest that the name was known even earlier in the second half of the third millennium. The name Ugarit is mentioned a number of times in the Tell el-Amarna letters, and in Hittite texts from Boghazkoi. In a letter discovered at Mari, which had been sent by a certain Hammurabi, king of Iamhad, reference is made to someone designated 'the man of Ugarit', apparently the king, who wished to pay a visit to the palace of king Zimrilim. This letter demonstrates not merely that the name Ugarit was known, but that there were contacts between Ugarit and Mesopotamia – a fact borne out by the discovery at Ras Shamra of several cylinder seals dating from the time of the first Babylonian dynasty and bearing Akkadian names.

It is also to the early second millennium that we must ascribe an influx of Europeans into the Ugaritic population. Some burials in the lower layers of level II contain ornaments of a style known to have had its centre of dispersion in the region of the Balkans and the Middle Danube. At this same period, the Hittites were settling in Anatolia, whence they were beginning to make raids further afield, e.g. to Babylon. The migrations of the early second millennium also included the Hurrians who were to establish the kingdom of Mitanni in north Mesopotamia. The Babylonian empire did not last long after the death of Hammurabi the Great, and gave way before the incursion of the Kassites from the Zagros Mountains.

However, the dominant feature of Ugaritic policy in the early second millennium seems to have been a turning towards Egypt, and, indeed, an increasing Egyptian interest in the region of Syria. The prosperity of Ugarit depended on its commerce, and this, in turn, depended on the land and sea-routes which appeared to be threatened by the growth of Hittite power in the north. In addition, troubles in Mesopotamia meant that there was a danger that Ugarit would be cut off from its links with that area. On their part, the Egyptian Pharaohs of the twelfth Dynasty may have feared a recurrence of what had happened earlier when the invasions of the Guti in Mesopotamia had sparked off population movements which led to an influx of Asiatic semi-nomads into Egypt aggravating the disorder and disunity which characterised the First Intermediate Period. They turned their attention towards the the region of Syria in order to secure their Asian frontiers and assure supplies of such materials as wood for which they relied on the area.

Such Egyptian sources as the Execration Texts (imprecations against enemies inscribed on pots or figurines which were then smashed to bring about the desired adverse effect upon the foe) and the Tale of Sinuhe (an official who was forced to seek refuge in the region of Byblos) indicate that Egyptian influence extended north of Byblos. That it included Ugarit is now amply borne out by discoveries on the site, and we may well be correct to assume that the rulers and traders of Ugarit would welcome these moves. Finds include a cornelian necklace bearing the cartouche of Sesostris I (1971–1928), and a statuette of Khnumit, the wife of Sesostris II (1897–1878). At the entrance of the temple dedicated to Baal were found the broken pieces of two sphinxes, one of which bore a cartouche indicating that they were sent by Amenemhet III (1842–1797). Nearby other Egyptian sculptures were found, including a female torso and a priest. The most notable find was a stele offered for the repose of the soul of one Sesostris-ankh. The stele (inscribed standing-stone) depicted the man seated between his wife and his mother-in-law, and described him as city-governor, vizier and judge. It seems likely that he fulfilled the function of Egyptian ambassador to Ugarit.

It is also relevant to note that the alliance with Egypt does not seem to have inhibited commercial relationships with the Aegean area, and Minoans established a foothold in Ugarit. Evidence of Cretan ware has been found, notably a baked clay cup, eggshell thin and certainly imported from Crete, found in the furnishings of a tomb of level II.

It is perhaps to this period that we should date the reign(s) of the founder(s) of the dynasty of Ugarit. Much later, in the fourteenth century, the kings of Ugarit used a seal which bore a reference to Yaqarum, son of Niqmaddu, King of Ugarit. In view of this, it has been thought that Niqmaddu I was the founder of the dynasty and Yaqarum I his successor. However, it is not certain that the Niqmaddu named on the seal was in fact a king, and there may be evidence to the contrary. A badly preserved tablet from the royal palace apparently gives the names of about thirty kings in two columns; the last name in the second column is *yqr*, and if, as K.E. Kitchen ('The King List of Ugarit', *UF* IX, 1977, pp. 131ff.) has argued, the names are in retrograde order, starting with the most recent king and working *back* to the founder of the dynasty, then Yaqarum would seem to have been regarded as the founder of the dynasty.

Not surprisingly, a complete change in the situation at Ugarit occurred when there was a dramatic change of circumstances in Egypt. The twelfth Dynasty was followed by a period of weakness and dynastic rivalry during which influence in Asia could no longer be maintained, and which allowed the infiltration and eventual subjugation of the whole land by Asiatic peoples known as the Hyksos, or 'foreign chiefs'. These events provided the opportunity for a party hostile to Egypt to seize control in Ugarit. The intentional mutilation of Egyptian monuments suggests that efforts were made to remove traces of Egyptian authority. These new masters of Ugarit were probably Hurrians.

The major development of the eighteenth and seventeenth centuries was the building of a new quarter to the north-east of the existing city. This suggests that Ugarit soon recovered from the turmoils of the change of power, and it in fact appears that the city entered upon a relatively prosperous period. In the new quarter the dwellings were grouped along straight streets, and were stone built; under one of the ground floor rooms was a funeral vault, rectangular in shape, the walls slightly leaning inwards, supporting slabs which formed a ceiling. A feature of the funerary provisions from this period was the great diversity both in place of origin and in style of the various items, providing clear evidence of the cosmopolitan nature of the Ugaritic population. However, the presence of Canaanite pottery shows that the Semitic population had not moved away. Noteworthy too is the number of weapons discovered in the tombs – daggers, blades, and bronze-plated belts – indicating the military preparedness of the population of this period. Among the weapons were found some short swords in the style of certain Mycenean daggers, implying that relations existed between Ugarit and the Mycenean world.

Towards the end of the seventeenth century, a large and impressive palace was erected in the north-western part of the city. Some of the walls of this 'Northern Palace' had a facade of large dressed stones. In this same area and from the same period was a building which had apparently been demolished to make way for another. This was apparently a sanctuary, and is noteworthy for the number of votive offerings found in a deposit there – several hundred lamps, a large number of vases including some of Cypriot origin, together with a quantity of replicas of the scarab beetle (a symbol of the sun in ancient Egypt), many bearing hieroglyphic inscriptions; the deposit also included a fine axe, and two bronze statuettes plated with gold, one representing a seated goddess, the other probably a priest.

Once more it was a change of circumstance in Egypt which led to a new situation in Ugarit. After the expulsion of the Hyksos by Pharaoh Amosis (1552–1527), his energetic successors of the eighteenth Dynasty sought to establish even more firmly the influence which had formerly been exercised along the Mediterranean coast into Asia. Tuthmosis I (1506–1494) marched northwards, and reached the Euphrates in a remarkably short time. The speed of this campaign must have taken the local inhabitants unawares. It is clear that Tuthmosis I and his successor, Tuthmosis II (c. 1493–1490), were intent not merely on renewing the old alliances, which must by nature have been precarious, but on a policy of territorial conquest. With the collaboration of the fleet of the *Haunebu* or *Fenkhu* (Phoenicians), Egyptian authority was re-established along the east Mediterranean coast, and Tuthmosis II was able to state that the Asian tributes were being submitted punctually and that no one opposed his messengers across 'the land of the *Fenkhu*'.

But the process did not stop there. Tuthmosis III (1490–1436) and his successors decided to organise the Mediterranean ports into a series of naval bases, to facilitate military transport and to provide centres for the restocking of the provisions of armies fighting inland. An inscription on a votive stele found at Karnak, dating from the time of Amenophis II (1438–1412) suggests that an Egyptian garrison had been installed in Ugarit, and that this garrison had met with opposition in the form of an insurrection which the Pharaoh had put down. Thus Egyptian policies were not entirely without resistance, and it seems likely that the opposition came from the Hurrian element in the population. Whereas the other non-Semitic merchants and the Canaanites could only profit from the Egyptian presence, the Hurrians must have realised that their influence was being seriously threatened.

Indeed, the significance of the Hurrian element should not be underestimated. Noteworthy is the discovery in the library at Ugarit of a bilingual 'dictionary' in which Sumerian judicial terms were translated into Hurrian. This was the period when the Hurrian kingdom of Mitanni had been established in North Mesopotamia, and Mitannian influence was felt mainly in the political and military spheres, as attempts were made to thwart Egyptian expansion and reassert Mitannian ascendancy. Despite the Egyptian victories, notably of Tuthmosis III, Mitanni was far from beaten, and continued to incite Syrian cities to revolt. At the beginning of his reign, Amenophis II had to campaign against the Mitannians, and it was on his return from one of these campaigns that he had to deal with the insurrection at Ugarit, mentioned above. But on the whole the Egyptian presence seems to have led to a time of security in Syria such as had not prevailed hitherto. This security is reflected in the fact that houses were built outside the fortified enclosure of the city, so that Ugarit virtually became an open city.

Such was the situation until the former enemies, Egypt and Mitanni, became reconciled in the face of the common threat of the Hittites. This reconciliation was to usher in for Ugarit such a period of flourishing that it is often known as the Golden Age of Ugarit.

Level		Period	Approximate dates
		Roman	First and second centuries AD
		Hellenistic	c.333–200 BC
		Persian	c.550–333
	3	Late Bronze III	c1365–1185
I	2	Late Bronze II	c.1450–1365
	1	Late Bronze I	c.1600–1450
	3	Middle Bronze III	c.1750–1650
II	2	Middle Bronze II	c.1900–1750
	1	Middle Bronze I	c.2100–1900
	3	Early Bronze III	c.2300–2100
III A	2	Early Bronze II	c.2600–2300
	1	Early Bronze I	c.3000–2600
III B		Final Chalcolithic	c.4000–3000
III C		'Ubaid'	c.4300–4000
IV A		Late Chalcolithic	c.4500–4300
IV B		Middle Chalcolithic	c.5000–4500
IV C		Early Chalcolithic	c.5250–5000
V A		Late Neolithic	c.5750–5250
V B		Middle Neolithic	c.6000–5750
V C		Early Neolithic	c.6500–6000

Table showing detailed stratigraphy of Ras Shamra. (Approximate dates of periods are taken from figures 901 and 902 in the article on 'Ras Shamra' in *Supplément au Dictionnaire de la Bible*, fasc.52–53.)

2

The Golden Age of Ugarit

Past centuries had seen Ugarit come under the influence of Egyptians, then of Hurrians, and then of Egyptians again. In the reign of Pharaoh Amenophis II (1438–1412) the relationship between Egypt and the Hurrian kingdom of Mitanni underwent a dramatic change. While the reconciliation between these long-time adversaries may initially have been due less to good will than to a shared anxiety over the threat beginning to emerge in the shape of the Hittites, the alliance between Egypt and Mitanni lasted many years. The successor of Amenophis II, Tuthmosis IV (1412–1402), married the daughter of the Mitannian king, while Amenophis III (1402–1364) travelled to Mitanni to go lion hunting; he also had a Mitannian princess in his harem. The Egypto-Mitannian alliance ushered in a period of peace for Ugarit which was in fact to outlast it, since even after the Hittites had conquered Mitanni, they did not immediately seek to interfere in Egypt's erstwhile coastal possessions.

This, then, was a particularly flourishing time for the city of Ugarit, as is shown by the size of the population, and the plan of the city with its spacious quarters of streets intersecting at right angles, and impressive houses. The city also flourished as never before thanks to its commercial activities which thrived on the security of the land and sea routes. This growth of commercial activity is reflected most clearly in the construction of an entirely new quarter of the city near the bay. The excavations have revealed not merely dwelling houses and burial vaults, but stores and large warehouses with many rooms. In one room were found over eighty jars neatly arranged in rows, leaning against each other, which would have contained oil or wine. In the same area was a building which held over a thousand vases, mainly of Cypriot origin, such as were used to export perfumes, suggesting that the cosmetic trade was highly developed; here, too, were found alabaster flasks and vases of Syrian origin but modelled on Egyptian designs, and ivory make-up boxes shaped like a water-bird.

Little has been said hitherto of kings of Ugarit, although we noted that the founder of the dynasty probably lived in the nineteenth or eighteenth century. Before the publication of the king-list mentioned in the previous chapter (p.38), there was evidence of a king Ibira(nu) whose reign could be dated towards the end of the fifteenth century, and possibly another Yaqarum; a tablet from Alalakh names a certain Puruqqu, who is described as 'man of Ugarit' – a phrase which elsewhere refers to the king, who may have reigned in Ugarit c.1700 BC. The king-list may provide the names of a number of the earlier kings of Ugarit, but the precise interpretation of the list is far from clear, and it is impossible to be certain about the dates of their reigns. It is in the fourteenth century that it becomes possible to produce an unbroken sequence of kings of Ugarit.

Early in the fourteenth century, the king of Ugarit was Ammistamru I. (The 'traditional' numbers will be added to the names of the kings in this section of the outline of Ugarit's history, although the numeration will be affected by the king-list and by whether Yaqarum or Niqmaddu 'I' was the founder of the dynasty.) That Ugarit lay within the Egyptian sphere of influence is suggested by the fact that one of the letters from Ugarit discovered among the Tell el-Amarna letters bears the name of Ammistamru, who declares his loyalty to Amenophis III and requests Egyptian aid against an enemy. We may also note here that other letters from Tell el-Amarna suggest that Ugarit remained loyal to Egypt throughout the reign of Amenophis III.

Niqmaddu II reigned in the mid-fourteenth century, and to his reign we shall shortly return. It may, however, be relevant to mention here Niqmaddu's successors. His son Arhalbu succeeded, but died young and childless; his will has been discovered, nominating his brother to marry his widow and succeed to the throne on his death. His brother Niqmepa came to the throne probably towards the end of the fourteenth century. His successor, Ammistamru II, married the daughter of the king of Amurru, a princess named Ahat-milki, whose dowry was one of exceptional richness. His son Ibiranu succeeded, then Niqmaddu III, and finally there reigned a king named 'Ammurapi. Whether this dynasty, which traced its origins back to Niqmaddu I and Yaqarum I, had in fact remained in power from its inception to the destruction of the city, or whether it had suffered periods of eclipse after which it had regained power, it is impossible to be certain.

It was probably in the reign of Niqmaddu II that many of the Ugaritic myths were committed to writing, though they may have existed in oral form for many years previously; the colophons at the end of tablets *CTA* 4 and 6 mention a Niqmaddu as king. To his reign, or that of his predecessor should be dated a great disaster which befell the city. The excavators believe that an earthquake and tidal wave struck, ravaging the city, destroying or seriously damaging buildings; this seems to have been followed by a fire. The palace was damaged, but it was the port area which was most seriously affected, and warehouses and workshops were so utterly destroyed that they had to be completely rebuilt. In a letter reporting the disaster to Pharaoh Amenophis IV, Abimilki, king of Tyre, said that the city had been burnt, and that half of the city was no longer there.

Another statement in the letter of Abimilki introduces us to the dominant feature of Ugarit's diplomatic policy; concerning Ugarit, the king of Tyre reported that the soldiers of the Hittite army were not there. With the rise of power of the Hittites, tension grew with the Egyptians, and the attitude of Amenophis IV/Akhenaten (1364–1347), which amounted almost to indifference, seems to have caused great concern to Egypt's erstwhile allies and vassals in the regions of Syria and Palestine. The letters discovered at Tell el-Amarna have already been mentioned. These were found on the site of ancient Akhetaten, the new capital built by Akhenaten in connection with his attempt to foster the worship of the solar disc, the Aten. These shed light on this troubled period, as various local rulers implore assistance from their former suzerain, or report uprisings and defections. In one of these letters, the king of Ugarit appears to be warning the Pharaoh that he can only ward off threats to his territory by sending tribute to the Hittite king. Other letters report that ships cannot be sent to Ugarit for wood, because the region is unsafe, and that the whole region had defected.

Niqmaddu seems to have found himself cut off from the possibility of Egyptian aid by one Aziru, king of Amurru, so made an alliance with Aziru; in return for the payment of a considerable sum of money, Aziru would lend Niqmaddu his chariots and infantry if Ugarit were attacked by an enemy. However, when Aziru entered into alliance with the Hittite king Shuppiluliumash I, Niqmaddu was forced to come to terms with the Hittites. Another factor which may have lain behind the establishment of diplomatic relationships between the Hittite and Ugaritic kings was the desire of Shuppiluliumash to count on the friendship of Ugarit, at a time when three nearby kings were in revolt; in these circumstances, Shuppiluliumash wrote to Niqmaddu, promising to reward him if he would favour the Hittite cause. In return for his assurance of loyalty, the frontiers of Niqmaddu's territory were guaranteed, and indeed apparently enlarged, but a sizeable tribute was imposed. One of the texts recording the correspondence between the two kings refers to presents of gold and silver, purple wool and vases, sent to the Hittite king and his court.

But this link with the Hittites did not mean a complete break with Egypt. Indeed, Niqmaddu seems to have married an Egyptian princess named Šarelli, believed to be a daughter of Akhenaten and Nefertiti. An alabaster vase found in 1952 bore a hieroglyphic inscription containing the name of Niqmaddu, described as 'the Great One of the land of Ugarit'. The vase also bore a scene depicting the king seated beneath a canopy, receiving water and a towel from a young woman; this picture is reminiscent of the Egyptian ritual for court marriages, and probably represents his wedding to the Egyptian princess. Thus Ugarit appears to have attempted to remain neutral, or perhaps it would be better to say that it seemed diplomatic to maintain links with both powers. The long reign of Niqmaddu (probably from c.1360 to c.1330) seems to have been a prosperous one, and Ugarit may have retained the position of commercial intermediary between the two powers.

In view of the spread of Hittite influence, it was clearly politic for Ugarit to pay tribute and acknowledge Hittite military superiority. Niqmaddu was succeeded by two sons in turn. First was Arḫalbu, whose reign was relatively short. This may have been due to the fact that he became involved in insurrection against the Hittites, or at least that he did not demonstrate the same fidelity towards them, for his brother and successor Niqmepa made it clear that he was placed on the throne by the Hittite king. Ugarit seems to have suffered the punishment of some loss of territory. What happened to Arḫalbu is uncertain but it may be significant that, as we have already noted, his will required that his wife should marry his brother Niqmepa after his death, so that the dynastic line could continue. Perhaps he knew that his days were numbered. Subsequently Ugarit seems to have remained loyal, and, unlike his brother, Niqmepa enjoyed a lengthy reign, perhaps spanning the last quarter of the fourteenth century and first quarter of the thirteenth. Ugarit sent a contingent of soldiers to fight on the side of the Hittite Muwatallish against the Egyptians under Ramesses II (1290–1224) when the tension between the two great powers brought them into open conflict at the battle of Qadesh (1286 BC). Nevertheless, there is no evidence that the Hittites actually occupied Ugarit. Indeed, Ugarit seems to have retained its role as a prosperous port, and may have afforded the Hittites such an important trade outlet that they did not wish to put the situation at risk by too much interference. A few discoveries which appear to be of Anatolian origin suggest nothing more than the usual commercial links, and a seal suggests the presence of a Hittite ambassador. The payment of tribute and the provision of soldiers may have enabled Ugarit to retain its sovereignty.

Despite these links with the Hittites, there does not seem to have been any break in diplomatic relations with Egypt. In the temple of Baal were found fragments of a stele, dedicated to the local deity, by an Egyptian royal scribe named Maimi who was given the title 'chief of the treasury'; this was clearly an important personage, and it is not impossible that he was an ambassador. The style of the stele and its inscription suggest a date towards the beginning of the nineteenth dynasty (c.1300 BC). A number of alabaster vases have been found, bearing the cartouche of Ramesses II. It is difficult to be certain whether this evidence of a continuing Egyptian influence reflects the fact that there was no interruption in the links with Egypt, or whether this is evidence of a speedy resumption of good relationships after a treaty between Egypt and the Hittites had ended tension. But after the treaty was concluded, Ugarit was able to return to a period of prosperity in the thirteenth century.

As we have already noted, King Niqmepa had married Ahat-milki, the daughter of DU-Teshub, king of Amurru; an impressive list of the ornaments, clothes and furnishings which probably made up her trousseau has been preserved. When Niqmepa's long reign ended, it seems that Ahat-milki controlled affairs for a time before her son, Ammistamru II, took charge of events. His reign saw Ugarit's autonomy maintained, and the links with Hittites and Egyptians continued; there are also documents which show that there were relations with the king of Carchemish. Mention was made in our introduction of the discovery in 1956 of the Archives of Rap'anu; it was in the reign of Ammistamru II that this Rap'anu played a role of considerable importance in Ugarit, and he appears to have been an influential person at court, charged with negotiations with foreign lands, and involved in quite confidential and delicate matters. His library, discovered within his large house, does not merely shed light on his official duties, but proves him to have been something of a scholar.

A feature of Ammistamru II's reign seems to have been his family problems! At the very beginning of his long reign two of his brothers plotted intrigue against Ammistamru and their mother Ahat-milki. It was necessary to appeal for arbitration to the Hittite court and the court of Carchemish, and the decision was that the two brothers should receive their inheritance share and be expelled to Alashia (Cyprus); Ammistamru was given the right to choose his successor.

Ammistamru's marital relations also seem to have been fraught with problems, and he divorced at least one and possibly two princesses of Amurru! The texts speak of a divorce between Ammistamru and Pidda, daughter of Bente-shina, king of Amurru. The verdict in this case was given by the Hittite king, and stipulated that her dowry should be repaid in full, and that the heir apparent, Utri-sharruna, must choose whether he wished to remain in Ugarit and claim the inheritance or return to Amurru with his mother; he appears to have chosen the latter course, for Ammistamru was succeeded by Ibiranu.

The matter is complicated by reference to a divorce between Ammistamru and the 'daughter of the Great Lady', a princess of Amurru. Whether this is the same or another princess is difficult to be sure, but the two cases do seem to be somewhat different. The 'daughter of the Great Lady' had committed some great crime, perhaps adultery, and fled home to Amurru.

Ammistamru refused to accept the assurances of the king of Amurru that the princess would not return to Ugarit nor engage in intrigue, and threatened to come to take her back; the king of Amurru reacted angrily, by sending messengers to Ugarit to demand that Ammistamru renounce any attempt to assert his rights. At this juncture, the Hittite king intervened, declaring that Ammistamru could bring back his wife and do with her what he chose, so long as he paid a ransom to her family. In fact, he had her thrown into the sea, and repaid her dowry.

Ammistamru was succeeded by Ibiranu. There is evidence of tension with the Hittite court early in Ibiranu's reign; the king was reprimanded for his failure to visit the Hittite court or to send messengers or gifts. Nor, apparently, had he sent a required contingent of soldiers, despite a Hittite request. We are perhaps to see in this evidence that Hittite power was beginning to weaken. His son Niqmaddu III succeeded briefly, but little is known of his reign. The last king of Ugarit was 'Ammurapi, who reigned from c.1225 until the destruction of the city. There is evidence that Hittite power continued to wane, and 'Ammurapi refused to pay the customary annual visit to the Hittite court at Ḫattusas.

The thirteenth century saw an increase in the number of people of Aegean origin in the population of Ugarit. This is reflected not only in the style of tombs, but also in the funerary findings, and their skulls which were of Mediterranean rather than Semitic type. Although there had been an important Aegean colony in Ugarit from the fifteenth century, they now seem to have become the class of property. This marked decline in the Semitic civilisation of the city, and almost complete absence of epigrahic materials has been seen as an indication that Ugarit's literary traditions were at an end.

At the end of the thirteenth century and the beginning of the twelfth, there took place an invasion of warlike peoples from the north and from the sea. Although they seem to have travelled both by land and sea, they are usually known as the 'Sea Peoples'. These peoples progressed along the east Mediterranean coast, and ultimately crossed swords with Egypt. The secret of their superiority lay above all in their possession of iron weaponry. Light is shed on this period by some tablets actually found within a kiln; that they had not been removed suggests that they represent the very last tablets to have been written, and they make it clear that danger was imminent. In these tablets, we see the Hittite king urging that a ship and crew be provided to transport grain to an area where there was famine; reference is made to an act whereby the king of Ugarit has been released from his vassal status, but still has certain obligations to his erstwhile masters. From Cyprus comes a request for a ship and supplies, but the reply is that there is no ship to spare, for while the Ugaritic fleet and troops are occupied elsewhere an enemy has plundered its coastlands. Other letters from the kings of Tyre and Byblos refer to maritime activities along the Phoenician coast, but the events described therein may not be closely related to the coming turmoil. The likelihood is that the Sea Peoples were responsible for the city's destruction.

To all intents and purposes, the existence of Ugarit had ended. There is a sense in which the invasion of the iron-wielding Sea Peoples was symbolic of a more general economic reason for the city's decline and fall. The import of copper-bearing minerals, and the manufacture of bronze tools and weapons, had formed one of Ugarit's most important industries. But now the Iron Age was beginning to dawn. Even before the invasions of the Sea Peoples, the city's population had probably begun to decline as the foreigners who had come to comprise the propertied classes at Ugarit began to seek the refuge of their homelands.

Although the history of Ugarit really comes to an end in the twelfth century, a brief post-script is required, since there is some evidence that the site was occupied in a number of later periods, though we are dealing with isolated discoveries. Brooches from the Iron Age, dated approximately to the tenth century, have been found. In the seventh and sixth centuries the highest point of the *tell* was inhabited, as is shown by the remains of buildings, and a small cemetery of sarcophagi, made of large stone slabs, which contained iron spears, bronze brooches and alabaster flasks. In the sixth century, Greek mariners used the nearby port, perhaps in connection with trading activities, and gave it the name *Leukos Limēn* ('White Harbour') preserved in the name Minet el-Beida. From this period comes a hoard of silver coins, some of which had been turned into ingots. Again there is evidence of an occupation in the Persian and Hellenistic periods, including a Hellenistic sarcophagus containing a number of rich belongings. Numerous Roman coins and other remains suggest an occupation in the first and second centuries AD. On the surface, Byzantine and Arab coins were discovered.

3

Everyday Life in Ugarit

The City in the Late Bronze Age

The city of Ugarit was never the centre of any great empire, but it does seem that we can speak of a kingdom of Ugarit, of which the city was the 'capital'. This kingdom probably comprised a fairly small coastal strip, stretching from the vicinity of Jebel Aqra (the Mount Sapan of the Ugaritic texts) in the north to the region of Tell Sukas in the south, including the headlands of Ras al-Basit, Ibn Hani south of Minet el-Beida, and Latakia. Its eastern limits were formed by the wooded hills which run parallel to the coast, separating the coastal strip from the interior, broken by the main river of the region, the Nahr al-Kabir, whose sources are near Jebel Aqra, and which flows in a south-westerly direction, reaching the coast just south of Latakia. It seems likely that at certain times the city controlled larger territories.

The city itself must have been dominated by its two main temples, dedicated to Baal and to Dagan, which, with the house of the high priest between them, occupied the highest part of the mound. A brief description of these buildings will be given later in chapter 5. The most impressive building, certainly for its size, must have been the royal palace. This magnificent edifice was constructed in a number of stages from the fifteenth to the thirteenth century until, at its maximum extent, it measured approximately one hundred and twenty metres by eighty-five. The original building probably comprised a number of rooms around two small interior courtyards, one of which was paved with flag-stones. By the time the palace reached its zenith, it comprised some ninety rooms, as well as six large courtyards and other small courts, some of which were paved. One of the courtyards is noteworthy for the fact that it contained an ornamental pool, measuring eight metres by six, surrounded by two tiers of shaped stones. Elaborate arrangements were made for the water supply. Water was collected in a well some distance away, whence it was transferred, presumably by servants, to a trough situated beside the well. Thence the water passed through an outlet hole into a subterranean channel some eighteen metres long, made of stone

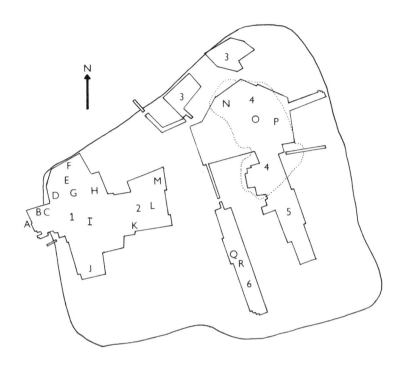

Key

1 Palace area
2 Residential area
3 Lower city
4 Acropolis (area enclosed by dotted line)
5 Southern slope of acropolis
6 Southern city

A Postern
B Tower
C Fortress
D Shrine
E Royal stables
F 'Queen Mother's Residence'
G 'Governor's Residence'
H Northern Palace
I Royal Palace
J Southern Palace

K 'House of Alabasters'
L Houses of Rašap'abu and 'the Scholar'
M House of Rap'anu
N Temple of Baal
O High priest's house and Temple Library
P Temple of Dagan
Q Public square
R Building with library

Figure 3   Plan of the *tell* of Ras Shamra, showing excavated areas, and locations of important buildings.

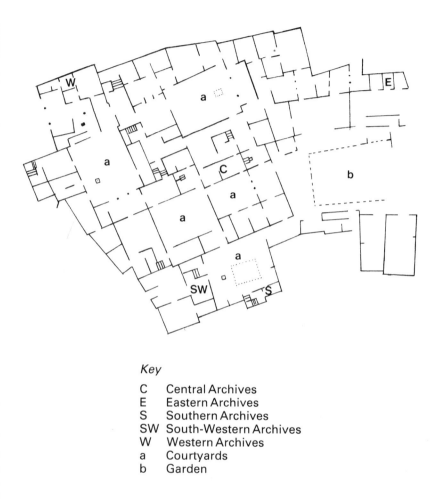

Key

C   Central Archives
E   Eastern Archives
S   Southern Archives
SW South-Western Archives
W   Western Archives
a   Courtyards
b   Garden

Figure 4   Plan of the Royal Palace, showing locations of major archives.

Plate 7   Staircase to upper storey in the Royal Palace

hollowed out to form a guttering over which were placed rectangular stone slabs, thus forming a sort of pipe with square cross-section. Another of the courtyards, in the eastern part of the palace, seems to have been an interior garden, comprising a large rectangular area bounded by a low wall, outside which was a wide path. It was in the north-west corner of this courtyard that the excavators discovered a number of pieces of carved ivory, including the panel to be described later (p.62).

The main entrance to the palace was approached by shallow steps and flanked by two wooden columns (whose circular stone bases still remain) which must have supported the roof. The palace was built of stone and is notable for the fine quality of the masonry and the craftmanship of the builders. Some of the exterior walls were buttressed with rectangular pilasters, while traces of plaster can be seen on some interior walls. A feature of some of the walls is a gap in the stone work where a course of timber beams originally formed part of the construction. A number of staircases led to an upper floor, which was probably where the private apartments of the royal family were located, while the ground floor housed guard rooms, reception rooms, store rooms, offices and archives. It is no surprise to find the king

Plate 8 Wall in the Royal Palace showing spaces where there were originally timber courses

of Byblos reporting that only the royal palace of Tyre could rival the splendour of that of Ugarit.

The growth of the palace reflects not merely the increasing size of the court, but the growing complexity of the bureaucracy of the kingdom. It therefore functioned as an administrative centre where official documents could be drawn up, sealed, and stored away in archive rooms. Here too were stored official letters received by the king, and translations into Ugaritic of important documents were made. Newly written tablets were baked hard in a kiln, discovered in the courtyard where the ornamental pool was located. Scribes learned their skills here, as is suggested by the discovery of writing exercises and glossaries.

The palace was guarded by a fortress, to which access from outside the city was gained by means of a small postern gate (see plate 10). Also in the vicinity of the royal palace were other major buildings, some of which almost amount to small palaces themselves. Indeed, two of these buildings have come to be known as the Northern Palace (which may have been an edifice of superior quality to the royal palace itself, but which seems to have gone out of use in the fifteenth century) and the Southern Palace. Further to the

Plate 9 Courtyard in the Royal Palace

north of the royal palace, at the very edge of the *tell* was a building which has come to be known as the Residence of the Queen Mother. Also in this north-west quarter of the city lay the royal stables, a building which may have been the residence of the military governor, and a shrine which was demolished to make way for another building. To the east of the royal palace was a residential area containing houses which clearly belonged to the wealthy citizens. The house of Rap'anu had over thirty rooms on the ground floor, and included a library containing both private and official correspondence. Other houses which contained a private library were those of a certain Rašap'abu, who was a collector of taxes, and of someone to whom it has become customary to refer as 'the Scholar'. In this same vicinity was the

Plate 10　The postern gate which gave access to the fortress area, viewed from outside

'House of Alabasters', so called because of the discovery there of about forty alabaster vases.

The houses often had an internal courtyard which would contain a walled well, surmounted with a small roof supported on four posts, and sometimes a trough into which water from the well could be poured. From a corner of the courtyard, a staircase would lead up to the first-floor level, which was where the main living accommodation was located. Another feature of the houses from this period was the presence of bathrooms and sanitation; the used water was channelled into cesspools, while rainwater poured directly into the streets.

The houses were furnished with subterranean funerary vaults where the deceased members of the household were buried. These would be situated beneath either the courtyard or one of the ground floor rooms. Carefully constructed, they are reminiscent of certain Cretan sepulchres. A typical tomb would be approached by a staircase leading to the main door of the chamber; the walls, sloping inwards, were surmounted with a corbelled vault; the floor was paved. The corpses were probably wrapped in shrouds and laid on the floor, surrounded by funerary equipment. Most of the tombs were plundered in antiquity, but since the robbers were primarily concerned to take precious metals, they left behind ivories and vases of faience and alabaster, often of Mycenean style, originating from Cyprus and the Aegean. Elaborate arrangements were made in some tombs to ensure that a drinking supply could be provided for the deceased; a pipe of baked clay, through which liquid could be poured, led down into the ground; a container would collect the liquid and a window might be cut opposite the container or a cup would even be provided to facilitate the obtaining of the refreshment! Similar vaults were found in the residential part of the port area, where we may presume the wealthy merchants lived as well as having their warehouses.

Not all the houses were so spacious as those near the palace. To the south of the temples of Baal and Dagan was an area of smaller houses, crammed together along narrow streets (see plate 12). Below this, on the southern slope of the acropolis, were workshops and houses with funerary vaults and sometimes cellars containing large amphorae. Nearby, in the area known as the Southern City, lived craftsmen and artisans, whose dwellings were built round a square, overlooked on the southern side by a large building which housed a library of texts.

The city must have been protected by an encircling fortification, but although some evidence of a wall from an earlier period has been found, the only hint so far discovered of the presence of a wall in the period under discussion is a glacis (a sloping earthen bank) which defended the fortress. It should, however, be noted that excavations have been concentrated on areas other than the perimeter of the *tell*.

Commerce and Industry

Our outline of Ugarit's history has already made plain the fact that its prosperity was largely due to the fact that its geographical location made it an ideal centre for trade. The rulers of Ugarit exploited its situation to the full. The city stood at an intersection of maritime and overland trade routes which made it a natural link between the Mediterranean world and the land

Plate 11   A funerary vault

Plate 12 A narrow street

routes to Mesopotamia and Anatolia. Ships from the ports of the East Mediterranean coast, and from places further afield such as Cyprus, Crete, and Egypt, would load and unload cargo. Trading caravans plying the overland routes would visit Ugarit.

However, the city's prosperity was derived not merely from its activities as a commercial middleman. It was, in its own right, an industrial centre where goods were manufactured and produce grown not merely for local consumption but for export. Metal workers had their foundries and work-shops not only in the city proper but in the port area. These metal workers specialised in the production of weapons and tools of bronze. In common with other places along the Mediterranean coastline, Ugarit was a centre of the manufacture of purple dye from the shell of the murex. Linen and wool were dyed, and prepared for export either made up into garments or in bales. The economic texts include a number which list various types of garment, or details of the distribution of clothes.

The economic texts also indicate that the produce of the land was exploited commercially. They include lists of vineyards with the names of their owners or locations, and details of types and quantities of wine; there was *yn ṭb* ('good wine') and *yn d l ṭb* ('wine which is not good') as well as wine for the soldiers and wine destined for Egyptians and Assyrians. The discovery of warehouses in the port area, some containing rows of jars, provide evidence of the export of wine or perhaps oil; again we note that the economic texts include details of jars of oil and differentiate between ordinary and perfumed oil. The ceramic industry was clearly well developed. Other warehouses provide evidence of a thriving cosmetics trade; one contained over a thousand flasks of Cypriot origin of the type used for perfumed oil, together with alabaster flasks and vases modelled on Egyptian designs but of local work-manship, and ivory make-up boxes. Grain, wood and salt were also exported.

In addition to providing information about the various commodities in which the tradesmen of Ugarit dealt, the economic texts provide an insight into the variety of trades practised. Corporations of silver casters and chariot makers are mentioned, and reference is made to a total of about a hundred trades. Not only are there lists of trades or corporations, but there are also lists of practitioners of particular trades, e.g. bow makers and ship builders. Other texts appear to provide lists of masters and their apprentices (*wlmdh*), and of taxes and wages; a text listing the names of watchmen under the command of a certain P'ṣ son of Byy bears the number ten, probably to indicate that each received ten shekels. As is to be expected in such a commercial centre, texts reflect the financial affairs of the city and include references to deposits, guarantees and interest.

The Law

The excavations at Ugarit have not yet brought to light a Ugaritic law-code analogous to such other ancient near eastern codes as those of Hammurabi, Lipit-Ishtar, or the kingdom of Eshnunna. Nevertheless, the discovery of large numbers of legal texts provides a window on the legal traditions of ancient Ugarit. The vast majority of the legal texts were written in Akkadian – the language of law as well as diplomacy in the ancient Near East. Most of the legal texts contain a single 'act', though sometimes a number of acts relating to the same beneficiary would be grouped on a single tablet.

It is possible to group the judicial texts into three main categories.

(i) Acts transacted before witnesses, characterised by the phrase 'before witnesses', a list of the names of the witnesses and of the scribe, and perhaps the seal of a private individual. These acts could involve such transactions as the making of gifts or wills to relatives, purchases and sales, the selling or freeing of slaves, and the repayment of debts.

(ii) Acts transacted before the king, characterised by the dynastic seal of the kings of Ugarit, the formula 'before A (son of B) king of Ugarit', and no list of witnesses. Such acts included purchases, sales and exchanges of goods, gifts to members of a family or other people, rules of inheritance, and adoptions. However, there is a considerable overlap between the types of transaction in these categories, and it is difficult to be sure why some were carried out before the king and others before private individuals; neither the status of the persons concerned nor the nature of the transaction seems to account for the choice, though we may perhaps surmise that those before the king were regarded as more solemn and efficacious.

(iii) Acts or decrees of the king, which, like the acts transacted before the king, are characterised by the dynastic seal, and the name of the king. There is some overlap with category (ii), but, in the main, the king appears as the bestower or remover of various benefits. Many of the acts take the basic form 'King A has taken away the goods of B and given them to C'. These 'gifts' could at times involve return gifts, so be classed as exchanges of goods; gifts could be made under certain conditions, or be accompanied by appointments or promotions. The king could absolve subjects of various burdens, liberate slaves, or reduce important people to the position of slaves.

The Arts

The high quality of the craftsmanship employed in the furnishing of the royal palace and other important buildings, the skill of the metal workers

Plate 13   Gold plate embossed with a hunting scene

who produced the bronze weapons and tools for which Ugarit seems to have been famous, and indeed the city's literary traditions all suggest that Ugarit was certainly not uncultured. Mention has already been made of some of the fine works of art which the excavations have revealed, and of the variety of influences which affected their design. Aegean influence, for example, can be seen in the representation of the bare-breasted goddess of fertility on the lid of an ivory box, as well as in various vases, goblets, heads and masks. Egyptian influence is evidenced by the bronze falcon with gold encrusted plumage, and cosmetic boxes shaped like aquatic birds. But this does not mean that Ugaritic art totally lacked originality, for the city was far enough from the great centres of culture for a local style to develop, despite the many clear outside influences.

Some particularly noteworthy examples of the art of Ugarit deserve special mention. In the course of the excavations in 1932, a gold plate and a gold bowl were discovered together (see plate 13). The former was embossed with a hunting scene – a figure in a chariot, perhaps the king of Ugarit, aims an arrow at a deer, while bulls flee before the chariot. The gold bowl was decorated with scenes which are probably mythological. While digging in one of the courtyards of the royal palace in 1952, the excavators came upon a number of ivory items, one of which proved to be of particular interest. This was a large panel, measuring approximately one metre by fifty centimetres, which must originally have decorated some large piece of furniture, probably a bed. The panel was in a fragile state, and had to be protected and allowed to dry out gradually before any attempt could be made to move it. The panel appeared to be composed of eight plaques placed side by side, each measuring twenty-four by ten/twelve centimetres, and two friezes. When the panel was removed, piece by piece, a surprise awaited the excavators, for a second panel appeared beneath it, and it became clear that the panel was double-sided, and comprised sixteen plaques in total; these, with the friezes, had been held back to back by ivory rivets. The two plaques at the extremities of each side of the panel depicted a tree, and between them were various scenes, mainly from the life of the king, including hunting and military scenes. We also see depicted the king with his wife, and a particularly striking plaque shows a winged goddess suckling two smaller figures.

The skilled metal workers of Ugarit needed to be able to weigh with considerable precision, and a number of weights has been discovered which suggest that both the Egyptian and the Mesopotamian weight systems were known in Ugarit. Weights were of various shapes, often geometrical, but sometimes for example in the shape of a bull. One particular find included not merely a set of weights but the two bronze pans of a balance, and one of the weights was intriguing for it took the form of a man's head with a rather prominent nose. Could this be a portrait of the metal-worker himself, and his way of identifying the ownership of the weights?

Plate 14   Weight in the shape of a bull

Plate 15   The north-west courtyard in the Royal Palace

The King, the Court, and Society

Clearly the king was the most important member of society in ancient Ugarit, and in every sense the master of the city. It is probable that one of the areas of the city's life wherein the king had a particularly important function was that of its religion. Indeed, it has been argued that the people of Ugarit believed in some form of divine or sacral kingship. It will be more appropriate to discuss this difficult subject in chapter 5.

We are on firmer ground when we turn to consider the king's role in society. There can be no doubt that the king controlled the political destiny of the city and negotiated on its behalf with the monarchs of other states. We have noted that he played a prominent part in the legal transactions of the city, and he was commander in chief of the armed forces. The ivory panel mentioned in the previous section depicts two marching soldiers armed with swords and bows, and, on the adjoining plaque, the king in military garb with crossed shoulder belts, apparently threatening to put out the eyes of a kneeling foe whose hands are raised in supplication. The palace itself and discoveries made within it speak of the king's status. Its size and luxurious furnishings – chairs of ebony, or decorated with gold and lapis lazuli (a dark blue gem-stone), beds and other items of furniture ornamented with ivory – show the rich life-style enjoyed by the royal family. This is further borne out by the objects of precious metal, ivory, lapis lazuli, and items decorated with jewels and semi-precious stones found within its walls.

That the queen shared the luxurious life of the king is shown by the accounts of their clothes and jewels which have been found. Notable is the trousseau of Aḫat-milki, as recorded on a tablet discovered in 1952, which included gold jewellery, bracelets and belts, vessels of precious metals, phials of perfume and boxes of cosmetics, as well as clothes and material. That the queen was not merely a consort but played a significant role at court is shown by the discovery of letters from important people requesting her intervention or mediation with the king in diplomatic matters.

The court was clearly sizeable. Various officials are mentioned in the texts, and although the precise significance of the title is not always clear, they seem to include a royal treasurer, a chief priest, a military governor, a master of chariotry, the mayor of the city, and an overseer of estates. There is evidence that others were associated with the court; we noted in our comments on the law that the king would sometimes direct the distribution of gifts to various dignitaries, and at other times he would deal severely with functionaries who abused his confidence.

The presence within the palace of a section reserved for the city's administration, shows that the court had an administrative function. Scribes wrote or made copies of the royal correspondence, and stored the many administrative texts in well organised archives. These texts show that there existed a highly organised system of fiscal control. The population was divided into districts, each of which was required to provide money or services for various royal projects. The texts also show that various families were grouped together into guilds.

High in the social structure of Ugarit were the military guilds or castes, and we have noted that the king was the head of the army and that his officials included a military governor and a chariot-master. The military nature of the society has been mentioned in our historical survey, and is amply attested by discoveries on the site. The city itself was well fortified, especially on the western side, nearest to the sea, where a fortress protected the city and its palace; it was perhaps this fortress which was under the charge of the military governor. The texts mention deliveries of large quantities of weapons. Breast plates were worn by archers and slingers and some of the chariot troops – scales from such breast plates have been found in the palace. The horses too were armoured with such breast plates, and the chariots were richly decorated. A text preserving a royal commandment for

Plate 16   Masonry at the north-west corner of the Royal Palace

the furnishing of two thousand horses underlines the importance of chariotry in the army of Ugarit.

Further reading on the city of Ugarit, its history and archaeology

M.S. Drower, 'Ugarit' in *The Cambridge Ancient History*, 3rd edition, 1975.
J. Gray, *The Canaanites*, London, 1964.
J. Gray, 'Ugarit' in D. Winton Thomas (ed.), *Archaeology and Old Testament Study*, Oxford, 1967.
A.R. Millard, 'Canaanites' in D.J. Wiseman (ed.), *Peoples of Old Testament Times*, Oxford, 1973.
R. North, 'Ugarit Grid, Strata, and Find-Localizations', *ZDPV* LXXXIX, 1973, (with re-assessment by J-C. Courtois, *ZDPV* XC 1974).
G. Saadé, *Ougarit: Métropole Cananeenne*, Beirut, 1979.
C.F.A. Schaeffer, *The Cuneiform Texts of Ras Shamra-Ugarit*, Oxford, 1939.
Article on Ras Shamra in the *Supplément au Dictionnaire de la Bible*, H. Cazelles and A. Feuillet (eds), fasc. 52–53.

4

Ugaritic Myths and Legends

It may prove helpful to those who are unfamiliar with the material if an attempt is made to outline some of the important myths and legends found in the Ugaritic corpus. This is, by nature, an exercise fraught with problems in view of the damaged state of many of the tablets, and of the frequently very fragmentary nature of the text which can be read. There is, in addition, the problem of deciding what relationship, if any, exists between two or more tablets which appear to recount the activities of the same gods or invididuals. Is it correct to speak of a 'Baal (and Anat) Cycle' of myths (as have some scholars), with all the attendant problems of deciding on the correct order of events, or should we be satisfied with the claim that we have at our disposal descriptions of a number of the activities claimed for Baal by his worshippers? Perhaps, in particular with the texts about Baal, the latter is the safer path, although it is sometimes possible to suggest that the events described in one tablet are followed by those recounted in another.

Although the same scribe, Ilimilku, may well have been responsible for writing the tablets recounting the deeds of Baal (and, indeed, those of Keret and Aqhat), it has been pointed out that the arrangement of the text on tablet 2 is very different from that on the others, and that tablet 1 could in fact be a summary of a collection of stories about Baal. It seems that the scribes did indicate which tablets were linked together by common subject matter by placing an appropriate heading at the top of the first column of the tablet, e.g. *lb'l* ('of Baal'), *lkrt* ('of Keret'), and probably *làqht* ('of Aqhat'). In no sense, then, can what follows claim to be an attempt to outline a systematic 'Ugaritic Mythology'. The aim is rather to indicate something of the contents of the texts.

The Conflict between Baal and Yam (*CTA* 2)

The story appears to revolve round rival claims to kingship. El, the head of the pantheon, instructs Kathir-and-Ḥasis, the craftsman of the gods, to construct a palace for Yam, the god of the seas and rivers. The god Athtar, who appears to be a claimant to the kingship, is told by Shapash, the sun-goddess, that El intends to grant the kingship to Yam. Athtar bemoans the fact that he has no palace or court, and that he will die alone, while Yam is to be feasted and have a palace. When Athtar asks why he should not be king, Shapash replies that it is because he has no wife.

In the meantime, Kathir-and-Ḥasis has apparently travelled to the abode of Yam, but threatens him with destruction and mentions the name of Baal whose claims to kingship he presumably supports. (Driver suggested that it is Baal himself who addresses Yam here.) Yam sends messengers to El and the assembly of the gods to demand that Baal be handed over. The messengers arrive while the gods are banqueting, and the latter are described as hiding their heads in their laps in fear. Baal rebukes the gods, and says that he will answer Yam's envoys. The messengers proceed to the presence of El, prostrate themselves before him, and deliver their message. El declares that Baal is their slave, but the sequel to this declaration is unclear. Driver saw a statement that Baal was gentle, but that he would be restrained if he threatened the messengers. Gibson sees a statement that Baal becomes enraged and has to be restrained by the goddesses Anat and Athirat.

When it becomes possible to follow the story again, it seems that the confrontation between Baal and Yam has already begun, and that Baal is getting the worst of things, so much so that he is on the point of submission. Having expressed his despair to Kathir-and-Ḥasis, he sinks to the ground beneath Yam's throne. (Driver suggested that it is Anat who first assails Yam.) Kathir-and-Ḥasis urges Baal not to submit, but rather that he must gain the victory and seize an everlasting kingdom. He provides Baal with two clubs which are given magical names (Yagrush, 'let him chase away', and Ayyamur, 'let him expel'). These clubs almost seem to have a life of their own, since they leap from Baal's hands and strike Yam, the first on the shoulders, but Yam does not fall, the second on the forehead. Yam falls to the ground, and Baal despatches him. Before the text becomes impossible to follow, it appears that the goddess Athtarat urges Baal either to scatter the body of his rival, or perhaps to be ashamed.

There follows a declaration, perhaps by Baal himself, that Yam is dead and that Baal shall be king.

The Building of Baal's Palace (CTA 3 and 4)

When the text of tablet 3 becomes clear, a banquet is in progress. A not uncommon view is that this is the celebration for Baal's victory over Yam. Joints of meat are carved and set before Baal, wine is flowing in abundance, there is singing and music, and Baal notes the arrival of his daughters. The precise relationship between this scene and the bloodthirsty episode which forms the next legible section, is not clear. Anat, having adorned herself, leaves her abode, meets her servants in a valley where two cities are situated, and falls upon the inhabitants. The slaughter is immense; Anat is described as decking herself with the heads and hands of the dead, and wading knee deep in blood. Still not satisfied, she returns to her home to set out tables and chairs for the soldiers (presumably those who have not been slain in the preceding battle), or, perhaps, the furniture is smashed on the heads of the soldiers. In any case, they too are set upon by the exultant goddess. The slaughter over, she sets about cleaning her home and offers a peace offering. The house is set to rights, and Anat cleanses herself with water, dew, and oil.

Baal describes to his messengers Anat singing of her love for him and for his daughters, Pidray, Tallay, and Arṣay, and sends them to pay homage to her. They are to tell her to perform a rite, then to hurry to Baal who has something of the utmost importance to divulge to her. The secret he proposes to impart is that of the lightning, which he is about to seek on his holy mountain, Ṣapan. When Anat sees Baal's messengers (Gupn and Ugar), she appears distraught, apparently assuming that some enemy has threatened Baal. She asks has she not herself slain Yam and other opponents of Baal. (This episode, of course, constitutes something of a problem to the view that we are dealing with a systematic Baal-cycle.) Gupn and Ugar assure her that no foe has arisen against Baal, and proceed to relay Baal's message. Anat appears to suggest that she will only obey if Baal will first demonstrate his powers to send thunder and lightning. She also informs them of her intention to journey to the distant abode of El. Baal sees Anat approaching, dismisses the women who are with him, and prepares food for her while she washes and adorns herself.

After a lacuna, Baal seems to be complaining that he has no palace of his own. Anat says that she will confront El, and, if he does not grant Baal a house like the other gods, she will drag him to the ground and beat him upon the head. She sets out for the abode of El 'at the source of the rivers, between the springs of the two deeps', and there confronts El. (A note here may suggest that the earth is being scorched by the sun.) She tells El not to rejoice in his own palace, for she will destroy it and injure him. El then asks Anat what she wants, and she declares that Baal is king, so is now pleading with El to grant him a palace of his own, as befits his station.

Although the text breaks off at this point so the outcome of the petition is not clear, the answer cannot have been an unequivocal 'Yes', for further steps have to be taken. Qadesh-and-Amrur, described as the 'fisherman of

Athirat', is despatched to Memphis(?), the home of Kathir-and-Hasis, where he is to pay homage to the craftsman-god, and pass on a message of Baal. Tablet 4 becomes legible in the midst of a speech which appears to be that of Qadesh-and-Amrur to Kathir-and-Hasis, and which includes an instruction to the craftsman to make a present for El's consort Athirat. Kathir-and-Hasis proceeds to smelt great quantities of gold and silver, and fashions exquisite pieces of furniture, a bowl, and a pair of thonged sandals.

Athirat is engaged in a variety of tasks – spinning, washing, placing a cauldron on the fire – and apparently thinking of her husband El, when she sees Baal and Anat approaching. Her immediate reaction is to be greatly disturbed, thinking that they are enemies intent on harming her and her family. But when she sees the silver and gold of the presents she rejoices and instructs Qadesh-and-Amrur to cast his net into the sea. The text is somewhat fragmentary, but, as they approach, Baal and Anat appear to be discussing his prospects of the kingship, and Baal recalls how disgracefully he was treated by the assembly of the gods. On arrival, they make their request of Athirat that she will approach El on Baal's behalf. Athirat asks why they have not approached El themselves, to which they respond that they propose to speak with El having first made their entreaty to her. They then appear to share a meal with other gods.

The decision of Baal and Anat to use the good offices of Athirat seems to have been wise, for (after a gap in the text), Athirat instructs her servant to prepare an ass for a journey. Accompanied by Anat (Baal having returned to Sapan) and her servant Qadesh-and-Amrur, Athirat journeys to the abode of El and pays homage to him. El enquires the reason for her visit, and whether it is for love of him that she has come. She compliments El then declares that she and Anat wish to wait upon Baal, whom she declares to be their king and judge, but cannot do so because he has no palace like the other gods. El's immediate response seems unpromising, since he asks whether they expect him, along with his consort, to act like slaves and do the building. However, he gives permission for a palace to be constructed.

Athirat compliments El for the wisdom of his decision, declares that Baal will now be able to appoint times for the rain, snow, thunder and lightning, and urges that word be conveyed to Baal. Anat joyfully bears the tidings to Baal who, in turn, rejoices, gathers the necessary building materials, gold and silver, and summons the craftsman Kathir-and-Hasis. A meal is prepared, Kathir-and-Hasis is seated at the right hand of Baal, who instructs him as to the type of palace he requires. There follows a discussion as to whether the palace is to have a window; Kathir-and-Hasis wishes to include a window, but Baal refuses, in the end explaining that he is afraid lest his daughters escape or that Yam may gain access.

Work on the palace commences; cedar is brought from Lebanon and Sirion (Anti-Lebanon); fire burns for seven days, melting the silver and gold in preparation for its use in the building. On its completion, Baal rejoices, sets things in order in his palace and kills animals and provides wine for a great feast to which the gods are summoned. Here the text becomes fragmentary, but it is possible that someone is making a speech; the few words which are visible have led some to suggest that perhaps reference is being made to the slaying of Yam.

The gods depart from the celebration, and Baal sets out to capture a large number of cities. On returning to his palace, he has apparently changed his mind about having a window in his home, and he informs Kathir-and-Ḥasis, who laughs and reminds him that he has said all along that this would happen. Baal makes the window, and utters his voice through it. At the sound of the thunder, the very earth quakes, people far and near are terrified, and his enemies take refuge in forests and caves, where Baal taunts them.

The seal appears to be set on his kingship. Seated in his palace he asks whether there is anyone who would rival him for power. Should any such rival appear he will send a messenger to Mot, the god of death, to ask the latter to devour him. He, Baal, alone is king of the gods, and supplier of the needs of both gods and men. The end of the column is very fragmentary, but may include a description of darkness falling.

Baal sends his servants, presumably Gupn and Ugar, to the two mountains at the world's end, which mark the entrance to the underworld; they are to descend to the abode of the dead and seek the muddy realm of Mot. They are warned not to approach too close to Mot lest he devour them as though they are lambs or kids. Baal reminds them that it is due to Mot that the goddess Shapash is able to scorch the earth and the heavens. They are therefore to pay homage to Mot, and report to him that Baal now has a palace. The remaining few legible words of the tablet may suggest that Mot is summoned to Baal's palace along with other gods.

The Conflicts of Baal and Mot (*CTA* 5 and 6)

The tablets which record the relationships between Baal and Mot (whose name means 'death') are rather fragmentary, so the attempt to provide an outline will appear somewhat disjointed. It is not impossible that the events recorded in these tablets are to be seen as a sequel to the account of the building of Baal's palace, which, it will be recalled, seems to end with a summons to Mot to come to Baal's palace, presumably to acknowledge his kingship.

Tablet 5 apparently begins with the concluding words of a message from Mot to Baal, which is relayed by Gupn and Ugar, to the effect either that Mot's appetite is vast, but although Baal has invited him to his palace he will only provide him with bread and wine, or that Baal is invited to the palace of Mot to partake of a feast which has been prepared; despite the fact that Baal has slain Leviathan, Mot can transfix him; the very heavens will burn up, and Mot will crush Baal and devour him. After a break in the text, someone is describing Mot, the effect he has on the earth, and Baal's fear of him. Messengers are sent to Mot to report Baal's words that he is Mot's servant for ever. They reach Mot's abode in the underworld, and their words cause Mot to rejoice.

In the very fragmentary passage which follows, there is perhaps evidence to suggest that someone, possibly Mot, is invited to attend a feast. In the next column, a messenger (or perhaps Mot himself) seems to have arrived to ask the whereabouts of Baal. Baal apparently then approaches the gods who are at a banquet. The opening lines of what follows are very fragmentary, a fact which is particularly frustrating since they introduce a section which is difficult to interpret yet which appears particularly significant. When the text becomes clear, someone is speaking, and referring to burying someone, or making an offering of a calf to the earth gods. The speaker then urges Baal to take with him his clouds, winds, thunder-bolts and rains, his daughters and his servants, and to travel to the mountains at the end of the earth and descend into the underworld. Baal obeys, but first he has intercourse with a heifer, which conceives and gives birth to an offspring. Is the significance of this episode that Baal is providing himself with an heir, or providing a substitute who will be devoured by Mot in his stead?

The final column of tablet 5 depicts two messengers arriving at the abode of El, to report that they have found Baal (or the substitute?) dead. El is distraught, and mourns, shaving his head and cutting his body, and asking what is to become of people now. Anat too searches high and low, and finding the body, she too enters into mourning. (This description marks the switch to tablet 6.) The sun-goddess Shapash is besought to place the corpse on Anat's shoulders, and it is buried on Mount Ṣapan; animals are sacrificed in Baal's honour.

Anat journeys to the abode of El, pays homage, and declares that the sons of Athirat (presumably those opposed to Baal) may rejoice. El asks Athirat to put forward one of her sons to be king in Baal's place. They agree that someone with wisdom, and who can match Baal's strength, is required. Athirat proposes Athtar, whose epithet is 'the terrible'; he goes to Ṣapan and sits on Baal's throne, but finds that he is (literally) not able to fill it. He admits his inadequacy, and comes down from Baal's throne to his own more limited sphere, probably that of irrigation.

After a break in the text, Anat is depicted as yearning for her brother, beseeching Mot to restore Baal to her. Mot retorts that in his hunger he had to search high and low until he found and devoured Baal. Shapash is still scorching the earth and heavens; time passes, and Anat, in her yearning, is still seeking Baal. She lays hold of Mot, kills him with a sword, then winnows, burns, grinds and scatters his corpse for the birds to eat. She then, apparently, reports to El that Mot is dead, and asks him to dream a dream as a means of discovering whether Baal is alive. El dreams of the heavens pouring down oil and the river beds running with honey, and rejoices that he can now be at ease, since Baal is alive.

El instructs Anat to say to Shapash that the earth is parched, and to ask if she knows the whereabouts of Baal. Shapash undertakes to search for Baal, while Anat is to make preparations to celebrate his return, or else the wine and garlands are to be prepared for Shapash herself.

When the text again becomes legible, Baal is apparently restored. He rounds on the sons of Athirat, then takes his throne. Time passes, and, in the seventh year, Mot complains about the treatment he has received, and demands the surrender of one of his brothers so that he may devour him; this will satisfy him and assuage his anger. The alternative is that he will consume mankind. The text is again broken, but resumes with Mot apparently having been told to consume his servants or even his own brothers. He returns to Ṣapan to confront Baal, and the two gods engage in conflict, their action being likened to various wild animals, until they fall exhausted, Baal upon Mot. Shapash warns Mot that it is useless to contend with Baal, and that El will not listen to him; rather, El will overthrow his kingship. Mot, in fear, acknowledges Baal's kingship.

The tablet appears to conclude with words addressed to Shapash, acknowledging her power over the denizens of the underworld, and calling upon Kathir-and-Ḥasis to act as her companion and drive away her enemies.

Baal and Anat (*CTA* 10)

This tablet is exceedingly badly preserved. Indeed, it is only the beginning of column ii and the end of column iii which can be read with any degree of certainty. Column ii contains a declaration by Baal's servants (presumably to Anat) that their master is not in his palace, but that he has taken his weapons and gone to hunt wild oxen. Anat flies to join Baal, who sees her coming, pays homage, and greets her, declaring that he will 'anoint the horn of her strength' and that together they will defeat Baal's foes. Anat raises her eyes and sees a steer (perhaps a description of Baal), then apparently departs. It is impossible to make sense of what remains of the column.

72

Column iii opens with a statement that heifers, an ox, and a cow will be born to Anat. Subsequently there seems to be a reference to Baal going to his mountain and taking his seat on his throne. The following lines are difficult to follow, though they contain several references to animals, and it is possible that the birth is being described. The presence of the verbs 'embrace' (twice) and 'cover' in the succeeding lines may suggest a reference to the embracing and clothing of the offspring. It then appears that Anat proceeds to Baal on Mount Ṣapan, to announce to him the birth of the animals. Baal rejoices.

The Story of Keret (*CTA* 14, 15, and 16)

King Keret's entire family has been wiped out. He has lost seven wives, who have died either from natural causes or as a result of violence, plague or storm. He has no heir, so his position as king is threatened. Repairing to his chamber, weeping, he is overcome by sleep, and in a dream he is approached by El who asks the reason for his grief and whether he wishes for a kingdom like that of the bull El, here described as his father. Keret says that he does not require silver or gold, slaves or chariots; all he desires is progeny. The god instructs him to wash and redden himself, to offer sacrifices to him and to Baal, and then to make preparation for a campaign in which all, including those who would not normally be expected to do so, shall participate. They will come to the city of Udm, to which they are to lay siege. On the seventh day, Pabil, king of Udm, will be so disturbed by the noise of his animals (perhaps because they are hungry after the siege, or else because they have been disturbed), that he will send messengers to offer Keret silver, gold, slaves, horses and chariots if only he will depart. Keret is to refuse, but demand Pabil's daughter, the beautiful Ḥuray, as a wife, so that she may bear him a son.

Keret awakes, makes the required sacrifices, and the preparations as instructed, gathers a vast army, and sets out on the quest. In the course of the journey, they come to the sanctuary of Athirat where Keret vows that if he is successful in obtaining his bride, he will give the goddess a weight of silver and gold in proportion to the girl's weight. The journey is completed, and events proceed as the god has foretold in the vision.

Tablet 15 is fragmentary, but apparently the first column of text describes the way Ḥuray will be missed by the people of Udm. Column ii includes a description of a banquet in Keret's house at which a company of gods arrives. Baal asks El to bless Keret; El does so, promising that Keret's wife will bear him eight sons, including Yaṣṣib, who will be suckled by the goddesses Athirat and Anat. Subsequently he is told that Ḥuray will also bear many daughters, and that he will be greatly exalted. The gods depart. In the course of time the offspring are borne; Athirat remembers the vow Keret has made and asks him whether he intends to fulfil it.

Keret gives his wife instructions to prepare a feast for the nobles of Ḥubur, apparently the name of his kingdom. She obeys, and, having carved meat for the assembled lords, begins to explain why they have been summoned. There is a break in the text, but the next column seems to repeat the description of the banquet, so perhaps refers to a second such occasion, or else the double narrative represents a list of instructions followed by the actual account of the feast. Here, however, the text suggests that the reason for summoning the nobles is to ask them to weep for Keret who seems to be near to death, and likely to be replaced on the throne by his son Yaṣṣib. The few lines of the final column which are legible seem to refer to this or another meal at which those present are invited to sacrifice on behalf of Keret.

At the beginning of tablet 16, one of Keret's sons named Elḥu says that once they had rejoiced in the life of the king, but it seems that he is about to die, and the very mountains are in mourning; can Keret really be one of El's sons? Keret urges his son not to weep, but to summon Thitmanat (the name means 'Eighth'), his sister, who will mourn; he must wait until sunset and, perhaps not to alarm her, pretend that she is invited to a sacrifice and banquet. Elḥu himself is to perform various actions apparently designed to secure the help of some deity for Keret. Thitmanat comes upon him, realises that something is amiss, but Elḥu as instructed, pretends that Keret is not ill and that they are summoned to a sacrifice.

After a damaged portion of text, Thitmanat asks how long her father has been ill. The reply is that he has been ill for some months, is near to death, and that she should prepare a tomb. She enters the presence of Keret, weeping and re-echoing her brother's words. Only the central sections of columns iii and iv are legible; these seem to describe the aftermath of a ritual to bring back the rains, which have presumably failed because of Keret's weakness, but which now return, and instructions to Elsh, the steward of the gods, and his wife, to go to the top of a building, perhaps to summon the gods to the assembly which seems to be the setting of the scene of the next column. Seven times El asks the assembled gods who will drive away Keret's illness, and, when there is no response, he declares that he will cast a spell, and appears to fashion something; here, unfortunately, the text is broken, but the word 'dragon' appears twice. Then El appears to address one Sha'taqat, perhaps the being he has created, with instructions to cleanse him.

El declares that death will be overcome, and Sha'taqat be victorious. She proceeds to Keret, washes him, and he opens his mouth for food. The victory has been won! Keret instructs Ḥuray to prepare a meal, which he eats, and then resumes his throne. Yaṣṣib, who, it had been thought, would succeed Keret, upbraids his father for his failure to fulfil his duties as king, and urges him to vacate the throne in his favour. But Keret is clearly back in control, and he curses his presumptuous son.

The Story of Aqhat (*CTA* 17, 18, and 19)

Daniel has no son. He therefore undertakes a seven day period of incubation, at the end of which Baal, taking pity, beseeches El that Daniel may have a son to carry out the varied duties expected of a son – to care for him during his life-time, and perform the correct funerary rites. El responds by blessing Daniel, making him potent so that his wife will conceive. When Daniel is informed what is to happen he is full of joy and able to be at ease. He returns to his home, and, for seven days, feasts the Kotharat, goddesses associated with childbirth. They depart, and Daniel begins to count the months until his son shall be born.

There is a large break in the text, amounting to two full columns. This gap presumably included the description of the birth of the son who, we discover later, was named Aqhat. When we are again able to take up the story, Aqhat appears to have grown up, and a bow and arrows have been promised to him. Daniel, seated at the gate of his city, spies in the distance Kathir-and-Ḥasis, the craftsman of the gods, bringing the bow, and he instructs his wife to prepare a meal. The bow is presented to Daniel, and the meal eaten; Kathir-and-Ḥasis departs, and Daniel gives the bow to his son, apparently urging him to offer to a deity, perhaps Baal, the choicest of the game he shoots.

The fragmentary opening of the next column seems to refer to a feast, at which Aqhat (and his bow) and the goddess Anat are present. The goddess covets the bow, and offers silver and probably gold for it, whereupon Aqhat retorts that she should provide Kathir-and-Ḥasis with the appropriate materials so that he may fashion a bow for her. Not dissuaded, Anat offers Aqhat immortality, but he responds that she is lying; old-age and death represent the common lot of all mankind, and he will share this fate. He is scornful at the prospect of a woman using the weapon of a warrior. Uttering threats, the goddess goes to El's abode, renders homage, and apparently protests at Aqhat's behaviour.

Tablet 18 contained only four columns, of which the first is imperfectly preserved, the second and third are lost, and the fourth in a reasonable state

Plate 17   Tablet containing part of the story of Aqhat (*CTA* 19 reverse)

of preservation. Anat appears to threaten El, and tells him to let Aqhat protect him. El acknowledges that Anat will not be thwarted, and tells her to carry out her plans. She journeys to Aqhat and begins to address him, at which point it becomes impossible to reconstruct the story with any certainty. In column iv, Anat enlists the support of Yatp(an) whom she proposes to turn into a bird of prey; a flock of birds will hover above Aqhat as he eats a meal, and she will join these birds and launch Yatp(an) against Aqhat. She carries out her proposal, Aqhat is slain, the birds devour his flesh, and Anat weeps, apparently over the unnecessary death.

Tablet 19 opens with a fragmentary section which may refer to the loss and/or breaking of the bow. There follows a statement which may imply that the fertility of the land will suffer or has suffered as a result of Aqhat's death. (Driver saw in this passage a reference to Anat's intention to restore Aqhat to life so that fertility may be restored to the land.) Daniel is again sitting at the gate administering justice, apparently unaware of Aqhat's death, when he sees his daughter Pughat approaching. She has noted what has happened to the land, and has seen the birds of prey hovering over her father's house. She weeps and tears her father's cloak. Daniel prays for rain, then instructs his daughter to make ready his ass, and he proceeds to journey throughout his land, embracing ripening shoots of corn, in the hope that they will come to fruition, so that Aqhat may place them in the granary.

Messengers arrive, weeping and lamenting, and announce that Anat has caused the death of Aqhat. The effect on Daniel is dramatic, as he writhes in anguish. Suddenly he spies birds flying overhead, and he begs Baal to bring them down that he may cut them open to see if he can find the remains of Aqhat. No remains are found, so Baal is asked to restore of the birds and they fly away. Daniel then sees Hirgab, the father of the eagles, who is also brought down, but no remains are found. But when Sumul, the mother of the eagles is brought down, Daniel finds the remains of Aqhat which he buries. Daniel warns the eagles not to disturb the repose of Aqhat, and he curses the inhabitants and the fields of three cities which were near the scene of Aqhat's death.

Daniel returns home, where mourners bewail the loss of Aqhat for seven years. They are then dismissed, and Daniel offers sacrifices to the gods, upon which Pughat (endorsed by her father) asks divine blessing on her as she embarks on the quest for her brother's murderer. She washes and rouges herself, girds on weapons which she covers with a woman's cloak, and sets out for the abode of Yatp(an). Her arrival is reported to Yatp(an), who orders that she be given wine to drink, while he pours a libation and boasts that the slayer of Aqhat will slay countless enemies of his mistress. Twice Pughat is given drink.

The tablet ends, but clearly the story has not ended. There is a reference to Daniel in *CTA* 20, but whether this tablet (along with *CTA* 21 and 22) has any connection with the story of Aqhat has been a matter of debate, and the relationship (if any) is uncertain.

The Rephaim Texts (*CTA* 20, 21 and 22)

These three very fragmentary tablets are sometimes associated with each other, because they have in common the fact that they all refer to an enigmatic group, the *rpùm*, to be discussed later (p.105ff). The texts have sometimes been referred to as the *Rephaim Texts*, the term being anglicized on analogy with the Hebrew word *rᵉpā'îm*. However, whether there is any connection between the tablets in the sense that they form a sequence, or part of a sequence, is far from certain.

Of tablet 20, only the latter halves of ten lines of one column (A) and the beginnings of twelve lines of another (B) remain. Column A seems to associate the *rpùm* with a feast or sacrifice. In column B, after what may be an invitation or instruction to the *rpùm* to come to the speaker's palace, they prepare horses and chariots, and, after two days of travel, they arrive on the third day at the 'threshing floors' and the 'plantations'. Thereupon Daniel speaks, but the significance of what is legible of his words is unclear.

Table 21 comprises the latter sections of some thirteen lines of a single column, while on the reverse there remains merely the end of one line. Some reconstruction of the surviving text is possible since it contains two identical sections, and this same passage also occurs twice in tablet 22. The recurring passage represents a summons or invitation to the *rpùm* by El to come to his palace, perhaps to attend a banquet. Between the two invitation sections, El apparently declares that he will travel to his palace, arriving on the third day.

Tablet 22 preserves rather more text than 20 and 21, amounting to just over twenty-five lines of two columns, the second of which is considerably better preserved. Column A again begins with El's summons of the *rpùm* to his palace, which is perhaps followed by a statement of others who are to form part of the gathering – *mhr b'l* ('warrior/s of Baal'), *mhr 'nt* ('warrior/s of Anat'), and *rpù b'l* (the name of an individual or perhaps 'the *rpùm* of Baal'). (Only the first of these terms, which have been variously taken as singular or plural, appears at this point in what remains of the text, but the reconstruction is based on their occurrence in column B.) The summons is repeated. Virolleaud reconstructed the lines which follow to give a description of the anointing and enthronement of Baal, to which the *rpùm* are presumably invited, and this interpretation is followed e.g. by Driver. However, the presence of the words *šmn*, 'oil', and *kḥt*, 'seat' (which occurs a number of times as a parallel term to *ksù*, 'throne'), is scarcely sufficient to enable the acceptance of such a reconstruction with any degree of certainty. A possibility suggested by the word *ydr* is that a vow is made. The summons appears to be repeated, then the *rpùm* mount their chariots and their asses and set out.

Column B opens with a section difficult to interpret, but thereafter it seems to describe a great banquet at which the name of El is honoured. The warrior/s of Baal, warrior/s of Anat, and *rpù b'l* are present, as are the *rpùm*. Great numbers of animals are slain and vast quantities of wine are poured out. The feast lasts for seven days. Just before the end of what is legible there is a reference to Baal, but his connection with the feast is unclear.

Shaḥar and Shalim (*CTA* 23)

The tablet is in a good state of preservation, each side containing a single column of text, comprising a total of seventy-six lines. A feature of the obverse is that the text has been divided into sections by horizontal lines; these brief sections seem to include sections of myths or hymns and instructions for ritual acts. The last few lines of the obverse and the whole of the reverse contain an account of activities of El and the birth of some deities; with the exception of a brief instruction to the reader (which is not ruled off by lines) the narrative is continuous. Since the relationship between the ruled-off sections on the obverse is unclear, as is the relation (if any) between these sections and the longer myth, it is the latter which will be outlined here.

The beginning of the story is particularly difficult to reconstruct. All that is reasonably clear is that El is on the sea shore and that he encounters two women. On the assumption that *yd*, literally 'hand', is here a euphemism for the penis, it seems that El becomes sexually aroused. He then kills a bird and sets it to roast on the fire. The significance of what follows is obscure; the two women tell El that the bird is cooked, addressing him first as husband, then as father, then again as husband, though Gibson may be correct in interpreting the passage as a sort of test; *if* they call him 'husband' they will be as wives to him, whereas *if* they call him 'father' they will be as daughters; they in fact call him 'husband', hence the sequel! He kisses, embraces, and impregnates them; they give birth to Shaḥar ('dawn') and Shalim ('dusk'). News is brought to El, who orders that an offering be prepared for the sun-goddess Shapash.

El has intercourse with his wives again, and they give birth to gods described as 'gracious', and as 'cleavers' of the sea. Word is again brought to El, and the gods are further described as sucking the breasts of the Lady (probably Anat), and as voracious beings having one lip reaching to earth and one to heaven, with birds and fish entering their mouths but never satisfying them. The wives and offspring are sent away to the desert, where they may live among the stones and trees. For seven or eight years they scour the deserts until they come upon a being who is described as the 'watchman of the sown land'. They request admission, which is granted, and they are told that food and wine are available.

Nikkal and the Kotharat (*CTA* 24)

This short text is written on a single tablet, whose reverse has the final section ruled off between two horizontal lines. It opens with an address to Nikkal-and-Ib and Ḥirḥib, described as 'king of summer', and a declaration that Yariḥ, the moon-god, has had intercourse, presumably with Nikkal, who has conceived. The Kotharat are informed, and apparently (for the text is damaged) invited to wait upon her at her confinement. There follows a description of how Yariḥ sent to Ḥirḥib to request her hand for marriage, in return for which he will pay a huge bride-price – silver, gold, jewels, vineyards and fields. Ḥirḥib suggests that, rather, he should act as intermediary in arranging a marriage with Baal's daughter Pidray; if Athtar (presumably Pidray's present suitor) is jealous, then he will arrange a marriage with one *Ybrdmy*. Yariḥ declares that he will only marry Nikkal, so the betrothal gift is brought, while the members of Nikkal's family prepare scales on which to weight them. The passage concludes with an address to Nikkal.

Between two horizontal lines there is an address to the Kotharat who are asked to attend with various substances, though the meaning of the terms is uncertain. Their favour is apparently being invoked on behalf of one *Prbht*, whom the Kotharat are asked to applaud.

Notes on the texts

For the sake of convenience, the tablets have been outlined in the order in which they appear in Mlle A. Herdner, *Corpus des Tablettes en Cunéiformes Alphabétiques Découvertes à Ras Shamra-Ugarit de 1929 à 1939* (abbreviated *CTA*), the official publication of these texts in the series *Mission de Ras*

Plate 18   A pendant depicting a nude female figure – probably a fertility goddess

Shamra (volume X, Paris, 1963). A source of considerable confusion in publications about the Ugaritic texts has been the variety of systems used to enumerate the tablets. Here we follow Herdner's numeration as well as order. The order is followed in J.C.L. Gibson, *Canaanite Myths and Legends* (Edinburgh, 1978), probably the most convenient transliteration and English translation of the texts. This latter volume is a thorough revision of Sir Godfrey Driver's work of the same title, published in 1956, which presented the material in a different order.

Other English translations include C.H. Gordon, *Ugaritic Literature* (Rome, 1949), H.L. Ginsberg, in *Ancient Near Eastern Texts relating to the Old Testament* (edited by J.B. Pritchard, Princeton, 1950; 2nd edition 1955), and T.H. Gaster, in *Thespis; Ritual, Myth and Drama in the Ancient Near East* (2nd edition, New York, 1961). Major portions of the texts are translated in J. Gray, *The Legacy of Canaan: The Ras Shamra Texts and their Relevance to the Old Testament* (2nd edition, Leiden, 1965). Selections from the texts are to be found in D. Winton Thomas (ed.) *Documents from Old Testament Times*, (New York, 1961), and W. Beyerlin (ed.) *Near Eastern Religious Texts relating to the Old Testament* (London, 1978). Mention should also be made of the most recent edition of the Ugaritic texts published by M. Dietrich, O. Loretz and J. Sanmartín under the title *Die keilalphabetischen Texte aus Ugarit* (abbreviated *KTU*), whose first volume (*Transkription*) appeared in 1976. (Text *CTA* 2 = *KTU* 1.2, *CTA* 3 = *KTU* 1.3 etc.)

5

The Religion of Ugarit

Our knowledge of the religion of Ugarit comes not only from the mythological texts but from the various lists of deities and sacrifices, and certain texts which may reflect rituals. In addition to the written material, the temples, stelae and statuettes, and other items of cultic apparatus may help us to reconstruct a picture of the religion of Ugarit (see plates 19, 20).

The myths outlined in the previous chapter have introduced us to the most important gods of the Ugaritic pantheon. Head of the pantheon was El, who presided over the assembly of the gods. His major epithets are 'king' (*mlk*), reflecting his position in the pantheon; 'bull' (*tr*), sometimes thought to show an original connection with fertility, but perhaps merely a reflection of strength; 'father of mankind' (*àb àdm*) and 'creator of creatures' (*bny bnwt*). These epithets suggest that El may have been the creator, although no creation myth as such has been discovered at Ugarit. 'Father of years' (the probable translation of *àb šnm*) is possibly a reference to the regulation of the seasons, or else an allusion to his great longevity. In the light of this last epithet and the fact that El is relatively inactive, it is sometimes suggested that El is a senile or at least an otiose figure. However, it is perhaps preferable to speak of a figure of seniority rather than senility; El presides over the divine assembly and has to be consulted before major steps can be taken, such as the building of Baal's palace, and he appears anything but senile and inactive in the Shaḥar and Shalim text.

El's consort was Athirat (the Asherah of the Old Testament, cf. for example 1 Kings 15:13; 18:19; 2 Kings 13:6; 23:4,6) whose epithets reflect the fact that she was, at Ugarit, associated with the sea (*rbt àtrt ym* – 'great lady Athirat of the sea') and that she was mother of the gods (*qnyt ilm* – 'creatress of the gods'). Prominent among the seventy offspring of El and Athirat were Yam, Mot and Athtar. Yam's stock epithet was *zbl* ('prince'), and his alternative name and epithet were *tpt nhr* ('judge Nahar/River'); an epithet he shared with Mot was *mdd il*, 'beloved of El'. Mot's other major epithets were *bn ilm*, 'son of El', and *ġzr*, 'hero'. Athtar's epithet, *'rz*, is usually translated 'violent' or 'terrible', though J. Gray suggests 'the luminous'.

Plate 19   Statuette probably depecting Baal

Plate 20   Egyptian stele from the Temple of Baal

Although there is one passage which appears to suggest that Baal was a son of El, there are numerous passages which describe him as son of Dagan. Dagan plays no part in the mythological texts so far discovered, though his name appears prominently in the lists of sacrifices to various deities, and he had a temple at Ugarit. It is likely that he was an Amorite deity, and his name, meaning 'grain', suggests an association with fertility. It seems, therefore, that Baal was not a member of El's family, and it is noteworthy that there is often opposition between Baal and members of El's family. However there is little evidence from the texts that, as some have suggested, there was a conflict between El and Baal. Rather, the texts may be seen as reflecting Baal's coming to prominence among the gods of Ugarit in addition to their having some functional use within the cult. Similarly the Babylonian creation myth *Enuma Elish* has a function within the Babylonian New Year *akitu* festival but also reflects the coming to the fore of Marduk, the patron deity of Babylon.

Considerable discussion has taken place over whether the story of Baal's periodic conflicts with Mot reflects the annual cycle of the seasons. This has been widely accepted and in many ways appears to be an obvious understanding of the story. Nevertheless, there are a number of problems over this interpretation, not least the fact that the text refers to the passing of seven years during which Baal was unable to send the rains. It has been countered that we should not confuse 'mythical' time with the actual passage of time on earth, but it is strange that a myth which seeks to provide the rationale for the annual seasonal cycle should not itself reflect that cycle. In any case, it could be argued that it was Baal's victory over Yam which guaranteed that he was able to control the waters and keep them in their appropriate place, and thus that he could send the waters as rains at the correct seasons. The story of the conflict with Mot, and Mot's periodic victories, could provide the rationale for the droughts which must from time to time have disrupted the normal seasonal pattern, and also provide the assurance that, should Baal fail to send the rains when expected, he would eventually return to do so.

Baal's major epithets reflect his prominent position among the gods, achieved as a result of conflict, and his fertility-bestowing powers. He is 'victor' (*ảliyn*), 'prince' (*zbl*), 'king' (*mlk*), 'judge' (*ṯpṭ*), 'most high' (*'ly*), 'lord of the earth' (*b'l ảrṣ*), 'rider of the clouds' (*rkb 'rpt*). He is also given the name Hadad, a well-known ancient Near Eastern storm-god. Closely associated with Baal was the warlike goddess Anat, who seems to have been regarded as Baal's sister. Her epithets describe her as 'virgin' (*btlt*), 'damsel' (*rḥm*), 'wet-nurse of the gods' (*mšnqt ilm*), and 'sister-in-law of peoples' (*ybmt limm*). It is noteworthy that in the Old Testament Baal is associated

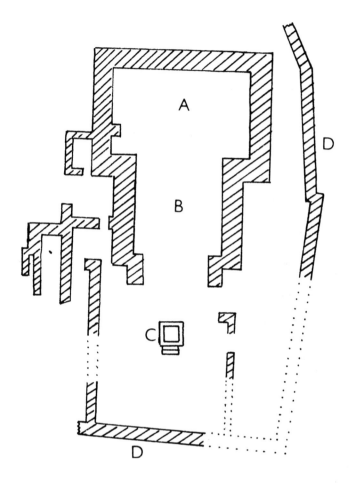

E

Key

A Inner sanctuary
B Outer room of sanctuary
C Altar in outer courtyard
D Walls of temple enclosure
E Location of discovery of the Baal
stele

Figure 5   Plan of the Temple of Baal

not with Anat but with Athirat (Asherah) or with another goddess, Athtarat (Ashtoreth in the Old Testament, cf. for example 1 Sam. 31:10; 1 Kings 11:33) who also appears in the Ugaritic texts, though she does not play any prominent role in the myths so far known; her association with Baal is suggested by her epithet *šm b'l*, literally 'name of Baal'.

A number of other deities play a significant role in the mythological texts. Noteworthy are the goddess Shapash, the sun, whose epithet was 'luminary of the gods' (*nrt ilm*), the moon-god Yariḥ, described as 'he who lightens the heavens' (*nyr šmm*), and the craftsman of the gods Kathir-and-Ḥasis, also called Hiyan, whose abode is perhaps to be located at Memphis, the home of the Egyptian craftsman-god Ptah (though this interpretation of the place name *ḥkpt/ḥqkpt* has been challenged). Many other deities are mentioned in the mythological texts, lists of sacrifices offered to various gods, and lists of the names of deities (cf. J.C. de Moor, 'The Semitic Pantheon of Ugarit,' *UF* II, 1970, pp.187ff.). One such list of gods, which was among the earliest published Ugaritic texts (by C. Virolleaud in *Syria* X, 1929), proved to be particularly interesting because of the subsequent discovery of a text in Akkadian (published by J. Nougayrol in *Ugaritica* V, 1969) which turned out to be an Akkadian replica of the Ugaritic list. Sometimes the Akkadian list simply transcribes and vocalises the Ugaritic (e.g. Ugaritic *dgn* appears as Akkadian *ᵈda-gan*) or translates a Ugaritic term; sometimes an Akkadian equivalent is given (e.g. Adad for Baal, Nergal for Resheph, Ishtar for Athtarat).

Religious life centred on the temples. Among Canaanite people these usually comprised an outer enclosure containing an altar for sacrifice and a standing stone, and the temple building itself which contained an innermost room in which the image of the deity stood and one or more outer rooms where various cultic activities must have been carried out. The acropolis of Ugarit contained two such temples; the larger and more dominant was dedicated to Baal, and its very situation may reflect his relative importance in the religion of Ugarit.

Baal's temple was identified as such by the discovery of stelae depicting Baal or naming him. Included among these was the stele dedicated to Baal of Ṣapan which was offered by one Maimi, who, as we have already noted, may have been an Egyptian ambassador. Other discoveries within the temple were bas-reliefs, fragments of statues, and Egyptian inscriptions among which was a cartouche of Amenophis III. Around the sanctuary were found sixteen votive stone anchors which dated from the nineteenth century. (We saw in our historical survey that the foundation of the temple is to be placed early in the second millennium BC.) The famous stele depicting Baal armed with lightning-spear and thunderbolt-club (see plate 21) was discovered to the west of the temple.

Plate 21   Stele depicting Baal armed with spear and club

Plate 22   Site of the Temple of Baal

The temple itself was surrounded by a walled enclosure. Within this, in front of the sanctuary building proper, was discovered what was probably the base of an altar which would have been approached by two steps. The temple was sturdily built, with walls 1.7 m thick. Entrance to the room which led to the inner sanctuary was by a large door approached by a monumental staircase which has been preserved in part. The inner sanctuary contained some sort of platform or perhaps altar constructed of large blocks of stone; this was approached by a flight of steps of which a single one remains. To the west were various rooms and passages, a bench and a cistern; it was perhaps from here that the cultic officials entered the courtyard. The sacrificial animals seem to have been led along a passageway which lay between the sanctuary building and the enclosure wall on its eastern side.

Close to the temple of Baal lay the house of the high priest. This was a large building with an open central courtyard surrounded by paved rooms; its walls were finely built of dressed stone. It was under the threshold of a door that the discovery of seventy-four bronze tools and weapons and a

Plate 23   The remains of the Temple of Baal

bronze tripod was made; it was, of course, the inscription 'chief of the priests' on five of the tools which identified the building. In three locations in the house were found collections of texts, notably the mythological texts. Some of the texts had the appearance of being writing exercises. This, then, was no mere dwelling house, but probably the place where the scribes would write out mythological texts, presumably (but see later) for use in connection with the temple cult, while the young apprentices would learn and practise their art.

Immediately to the east of the high-priest's house was a temple, thought to have been dedicated to Dagan on the basis of two stelae found outside its southern facade; these bore inscriptions which were recognised as dedications to this god. Although only the foundations remain, they suggest that the basic plan of the sanctuary was similar to that of the temple of Baal. They also suggest that the walls were remarkably thick – between four and five metres. This has given rise to the speculation that some esoteric form of cult was practised there, but this must be highly uncertain. Outside the south-east angle of the temple were found approximately fifteen troughs which may possibly have been for libations. It is, however, possible that they had no direct connection with the temple, but represent the remains of a watering place.

That the offering of sacrifices was a central feature of the cult is suggested not merely by the discovery of altars but by the texts which list the various sacrifices offered to particular deities. Considerable stress has been placed on the fact that there are several parallels between Ugaritic and Hebrew sacrificial terminology.

Plate 24   Stele with a dedication to Dagan

Plate 25   An altar with a pillar

UGARITIC	HEBREW
dbḥ (sacrifice)	zebaḥ (sacrifice)
mtn (gift)	mattān (gift(s))
mnḥ (offering)	minḥāh (offering, tribute)
ndr (vow)	neder (vow)
šlm(m) (peace offerings/ communal meal)	šᵉlāmîm (peace offerings)
kll (whole offering)	kālîl (whole offering/ holocaust)
nsk (libation)	nesek (drink-offering)
šrp (burnt offering) corresponds to	ʿôlāh (burnt offering)

But we should be wary of assuming that the precise meaning and usage of the terms was the same in Ugarit and Israel, and it is perhaps safer to believe that we are here dealing with a common stock of West Semitic vocabulary wherein there would be considerable similarity of usage, but local differences might occur. Texts have been discovered which indicate that there were appropriate sacrifices for special occasions or particular days of the month. Others list offerings to a particular deity, or sacrifices to various deities. Several different types of animal are mentioned in connection with sacrifices – oxen, sheep, lambs, kids, various sorts of gazelle, as well as birds. There are terms which denote the quality of the animal – gdlt and dqt referring to large and small female cattle respectively, tm ('perfect') and nkbd ('approved'). In addition to animal offerings, reference is made to vegetable and liquid offerings of wine and honey.

Perhaps the most graphic description of a sacrifice which has come down to us is that which is found in the Keret story, when he is instructed to perform a sacrifice prior to setting out on his quest for a wife. Keret washes and makes himself red, presumably a rite of purification, and perhaps we are to imagine that the reddening is achieved with the blood of a sacrificial animal. Taking animals, a bird, wine and honey he mounts a tower and makes his offerings to the gods. (This recalls the remains of a stairway noted above in the Temple of Baal which presumably led to a platform or tower where sacrifices were performed.)

An additional point deserves to be made about the Ugaritic sacrificial system, namely that no evidence has been discovered of the practice of human sacrifice. The impression has sometimes been given that Canaanite religion represented all that was bad and debased in cultic practice, and it is often assumed that this included human, and particularly child, sacrifice. It is true that the Old Testament contains a number of references to the

94

causing of sons and daughters to go through the fire 'to Molech/as an offering' in contexts where it is clear that an act of apostasy is being committed (Lev. 18:21; 2 Kings 23:10; and Jer. 32:35 where the act is associated with the erection of high places of Baal). We read that Mesha, king of Moab, offered up his son 'upon the wall' as a burnt offering in an attempt to turn the tide of battle (2 Kings 3:27); but there is no evidence to suggest that such practices were current at Ugarit. It is, of course, likely that a number of stipulations in the Old Testament are directed against Canaanite sacrificial customs. Probably the illustration of this most frequently used is the instruction, 'You shall not boil a kid in its mother's milk' (Ex. 23:19), in view of a statement in the Shaḥar and Shalim text which has been taken to mean, 'Cook a kid in milk' (so Gordon and Driver). However, the text is unclear at this point, and even if the suggested reconstruction $ṭb(ḥ g)d bḥlb$ is correct, it is uncertain whether the sense 'cook' can be justified rather than 'butcher, slaughter'. Nor is there any reference in the Ugaritic text to the kid's mother. This particular 'parade example' should be treated with some caution.

The reference above to the sacrifice offered by Keret reminds us of the fact that the king seems to have played an important part in the cult. It is appropriate in this context that some thought should be given to the view that the kings of Ugarit were believed to be something much more than the most important members of society with a prominent cultic role, and that the people of Ugarit believed in some form of divine or sacral kingship. Such views are often based heavily on the figures of Keret and Daniel, and it is important to note at the outset that although they appear to be earthly beings there are certain points which give rise to questions about their exact nature. In both stories, especially that of Daniel, there is constant interplay between the human and the divine. Yaṣṣib, Keret's son, is described as one who will be suckled by the goddesses Athirat and Anat, and both Keret and Daniel are called sons of El. Nevertheless, both are seen carrying out earthly pursuits – Keret makes an expedition to obtain a wife, and Daniel performs the functions of an earthly judge.

Several times in the Keret story, the god El is given the epithet $àb\ àdm$, 'father of mankind', which raises the question whether he was father of Keret (and Daniel) merely in the same way that he was the father of all men. Nevertheless, the stories suggest that Keret and Daniel's relationship to the gods was something different from that of ordinary mortals. The texts make it explicit that Keret was a king, and while this is nowhere clearly stated of Daniel, there is, for example, a passage where a curse is uttered by a king where it is likely that Daniel is the speaker.

If we look at the situation in some other ancient Near Eastern societies, we note that in Egypt the Pharaoh was thought to be the son of the sun-god, Amun-Re, in a physical sense; the god, to ensure that the proper divine rule of the land continued, made visits to the earth to beget rulers. The situation in Mesopotamia was somewhat different. Babylonian and Assyrian statements describe the king as a son of a god or goddess; Hammurabi, for example, declares himself to be son of Sin, Dagan, and Marduk, therefore this sonship was not understood physically but, rather, in some symbolic way. In Israel, the king was spoken of as a son of Yahweh (cf. 2 Sam. 7:14; Ps. 89:26f.). However, this sonship of the Israelite king was not physical, as is made clear by Psalm 2:7, where the word 'today' shows that the king was adopted on a particular day as Yahweh's son, perhaps his coronation when, after his anointing, the king stood in a peculiarly intimate relationship to Yahweh. In addition to being designated 'son' of Yahweh, the Israelite king undertook the role of 'servant', and Psalm 89:20 links this title with anointing. Here it is noteworthy that in the Ugaritic texts both Keret and Daniel are called 'servant' (*'bd*) of El in passages where the close relationship between the king and El is seen. In one, El has appeared to Keret in a dream to give him instructions as to how he is to set about the quest for a new wife; in the other, although it is not clear whether the birth of Aqhat, Daniel's son, is foretold to his father in a dream, (Baal appears to come to the latter while he is in his bed), the birth follows the intervention of El, at the instigation of Baal.

There is a passage in the story of Keret which suggests a belief that kingship depended on personal ability and physical prowess. When Keret is lying seriously ill, his son makes the following accusation against and demands of his ailing father,

> You have been brought down by the collapse of your power.
> You do not judge the cause of the widow;
> you do not try the case of the wretched;
> you do not put down those who despoil the child of the poor.
> You do not feed the orphan before you, nor the widow behind you, because/when you are brother to a bed of sickness, friend to a bed of plague.
> Come down from your kingship that I may be king,
> from (the throne of) your dominion that I may sit on it.
>
> (*CTA* 16 vi 32ff.)

The implication may be that it was felt that the king should be an outstanding specimen of manhood (cf. 1 Sam. 9:2; 16:12; 1 Kings 1:6b).

However, we have to look deeper than this and consider the suggestion that some form of divine or sacral kingship was practised in Ugarit, and that

96

there were festivals in which the king took the role of the god in ritual drama. Some would go further and find the themes which J.G. Frazer, in his *Golden Bough*, found at the very roots of the origin of the concept of kingship, namely that the fertility and strength of the nation were bound up with the sexual and physical powers of the king. It is, however, necessary to stress that a suggestion that the king took the role of the god in ritual drama is very different from a belief that the king was actually thought to be divine, and identified with the god. The two concepts do not necessarily go together, though some have felt this to be the case in Ugarit. The belief that the king actually played the role of the god Baal in the cult has been the subject of considerable debate, and depends to some extent on our judgement as to the precise nature of the mythological texts, to be discussed shortly. We must, however, ask whether there is any real evidence from the Ugaritic texts that the king was in any sense thought to be divine.

It is important to recall what we said earlier about Keret and Daniel, namely that they may have been something more than ordinary mortals. It is therefore difficult to decide how much weight to put upon these words of Keret's son Yaṣṣib as evidence of what was generally believed about kings,

Or do gods die? The progeny of Lutpan (a name of El – the reference is therefore to Keret as a son of El) shall surely live (*CTA* 16 ii 105f.).

It is possible to interpret these lines as implying that Keret at least was thought to be in some way divine, though J. Gray ('Sacral Kingship in Ugarit,' *Ugaritica* VI, p.293) suggests that we should not overpress the significance of this exclamation, which he takes rather as an illustration of the development of popular reverence for the king. If any such identification between the king and the god as has sometimes been suggested did in fact exist in Ugarit, we should expect to find some textual or inscriptional evidence. A possible hint at such a belief is to be found in the list of the kings of Ugarit mentioned in our historical survey. Each of the kings' names is preceded by the word 'god'. However, the list is perhaps to be understood as implying that the kings were deified after their deaths, and need not suggest that they were thought to be divine while living.

A feature of sacral kingship was the belief that the flourishing of the nation was, in some way, dependent on the physical well-being of the king. We have already noted that there is evidence that in early times the king was (or was idealized as) the most outstanding, mighty and able member of society. In the Ugaritic texts, the incident wherein Athtar attempts to take over the throne after Baal has descended into the underworld (*CTA* 6 i 32ff.) suggests that a similar belief about what was required of the king, physically, was held. We are told that when Athtar sat on Baal's throne,

> His feet did not reach the stool,
> his head did not reach its top (lines 59ff.).

It has been suggested that the inference is that Athtar was not fullgrown, and therefore not fit to be king. However, it is noteworthy that Athtar's epithet is '*rz*, 'terrible', which may imply that he was not a youngster, and in any case the passage which describes his descent from the throne of Baal appears (before the text becomes impossible to follow) to tell us that Athtar became king of a more limited domain on the earth. The implication is therefore not that he was too young to be king, but that he did not have the physical requirements to fill Baal's throne; while capable of exercising his own limited authority he did not measure up to the requirements for Baal's kingship.

We must therefore consider the possibility that any diminishing of the king's physical powers was believed to have some adverse effect over and above its natural limitations on his ability to rule. We have already noted the words of Yaṣṣib to his father Keret, where the latter is upbraided for remaining on the throne when he is ill, and his powers are failing. Yaṣṣib appears to suggest that Keret ought to abdicate the throne in his favour, rather than wait until he dies. The inference is therefore possible that the death of a king was thought to be an undesirable occurrence and that there was a practice of replacing an ageing monarch with a young, virile heir. It is possible that at the beginning of Yaṣṣib's speech, the word *ydk*, which we have translated 'your power' (literally 'your hand'), is, as elsewhere, a euphemism for the male organ, and that the suggestion is that Keret's virility is declining with his physical strength. We should also note that the implication of what is legible of the badly preserved column of *CTA* 16 is perhaps that Keret's illness has caused drought and famine in the land. It is therefore a possibility that a king's loss of physical prowess might have been thought to have some adverse effect on the flourishing of the land. But the evidence for this is slight, and indeed the whole subject of the religious importance of the kings of Ugarit remains one of great perplexity.

Although the king may have had a prominent cultic role, the texts refer to various cultic personnel and functionaries who were doubtless responsible for the day to day affairs of the cult. Mention has already been made of the *rb khnm*, the chief of the priests, and there are many references to priests in general. The chief priest is also called *rb nqdm*, and these *nqdm* may have been officials in charge of the temple flocks (cf. 2 Kings 3:4 where the term *nōqēḏ* is used of Mesha, king of Moab, and usually interpreted to mean that he was a sheep-breeder, and Amos 1:1 where the description of Amos as being from among the *nōqᵉdîm* at Tekoa has given rise to much discussion as to the precise nature of the prophet's occupation before his call). References are found to *qdšm*, literally 'holy/consecrated ones', and perhaps a class of priests, though the Old Testament parallel might suggest that these were male cult prostitutes, and to '*rbm*, literally 'enterers' who appear to be cultic personnel, and whose title is perhaps to be associated with the Akkadian phrase 'he who enters the house' (*ērib biti*), a designation of a particular class of priest who might enter particular parts of the temple.

Mention is also made of *šrm*, 'singers' – a fact which leads us to suspect that psalmody must have played a part in the religion of Ugarit. In the introduction to the first volume of his commentary on the Psalter, published in 1965, M. Dahood remarked that no psalms as such had yet been discovered at Ras Shamra. However, some qualification of this statement is necessary since there *are* texts which have been thought to be hymnic. It has been suggested that text RS 24.252, published in *Ugaritica* V, and particularly the reverse of the tablet, is perhaps to be interpreted as a prayer or hymn to various deities; K-H. Bernhardt entitles his translation of text *CTA* 30 (in W. Beyerlin (ed.) *Near Eastern Religious Texts relating to the Old Testament*) as a 'Prayer-song to El and the assembly of the gods', though the text has been differently understood and is particularly difficult to interpret.

The discovery of clay models of livers and lungs suggests the practice of divination in Ugarit, and there are episodes in the mythological texts which are perhaps to be interpreted in the light of divinatory practices. Keret receives divine instructions in a dream, while Daniel perhaps undergoes a period of ritual incubation before receiving a message from the god Baal. Also within the Aqhat story there is an enigmatic reference to Daniel's daughter Pughat as one 'who knows the courses of the stars'; this could perhaps be a reference to astrology, though Gibson takes the meaning to be that she is skilled in spells connected with midwifery.

We indicated earlier that the Ugaritic texts contain some evidence that particular sacrifices were offered on certain days of the month or special occasions. There are also texts which perhaps refer to other rituals to be performed on particular days or times of the year, but these are largely fragmentary and difficult to interpret. Therefore, when we turn to consider whether we are in a position to speculate about the nature of the religious festivals of ancient Ugarit, we must admit that we have to rely largely on the mythological texts, and that this raises the prior question of the relationship between these texts and the cult. It is therefore in order that we should discuss briefly the nature of these texts. The terms 'myths', 'epics', and 'legends' have all frequently been employed, and the discussion as to which is more appropriate has often revolved round whether the protagonists are predominantly divine or human. Other more detailed designations have been used; J. Aistleitner published his German translation of the texts under the title *Die Mythologischen und Kultischen Texte aus Ras Schamra* (i.e. 'The Mythological and Cultic Texts from Ras Shamra', Budapest, 1964) while S.H. Hooke ('Myth and Ritual Reconsidered' in *The Siege Perilous*, London, 1956, p.178) spoke of 'ritual myths'. These two designations introduce an important feature, namely an association with the cult. In this connection, A.S. Kapelrud (*Baal in the Ras Shamra Texts*, Copenhagen, 1952, pp. 14f., 17ff.) has stressed the significance of the place in which the texts were found, i.e. the library in the house of the high priest where the texts were copied and stored, and where, doubtless, young priests were instructed; the library was situated between the two temples of Baal and Dagan, which suggests that the religious texts were intended for temple use. Kapelrud noted that, 'A temple needed its cult texts, and cult texts need a temple', and saw it as more than coincidence that the god of one of the temples, Baal, is the hero of a number of the texts, and that a prominent feature of the Baal stories is the building of a temple in his honour.

Granted that the association between the texts and the cult is correct, what use was made of the texts in the cult? They have been described as liturgies, and it has been argued that the stories were enacted as they were recited; the spoken word would have a creative power which would increase the efficacy of the ritual act. The designation of the texts as 'cult drama' has been associated notably with several Scandinavian scholars. For example, F.F. Hvidberg (*Weeping and Laughter in the Old Testament*, London and Copenhagen, 1962, p.53) speaks of the texts as a 'recipe' for a cultic drama – a 'record of words and actions as they took place at the festival'. I. Engnell (*Studies in Divine Kingship in the Ancient Near East*, Oxford, 1967, p.104) argued that it is not surprising that the texts do not contain directions as to who has to speak or act as this would be part of the 'living tradition' and would not need special mention; he felt that the texts ought rightly to be called 'cult-rituals'.

The suggestion that there is a close connection between the texts and the cult has, then, received widespread acceptance from those who have given close attention to the texts. It ought, however, to be remembered that while the bulk of the literary tablets, including the Baal, Keret and Aqhat texts were found in the library of the high priest, a number of mythological fragments were found in other places with no connection with any cultic installation, and it is possible that people might have kept such texts in their private houses. Nevertheless, the very fact that texts which tell of the gods and their activities were found in close proximity to a temple suggests that we are dealing with a literature associated in some way with the temple. This suggestion is enhanced by the fact that the texts which give prominence to Baal and the great acts with which he was credited, were found near the temple dedicated to Baal.

If we are prepared to accept that we are dealing with a literature associated with the temple, we must still ask what was the use to which the texts were put. At the very least, we must assume that the writing was to preserve the memory of the contents, for there are clear indications that we are not merely dealing with writing exercises. One such indication is perhaps to be seen in the presence at the end of some of the tablets of a colophon. While the precise sense of the fullest colophon (at the end of the tablet telling of the conflict between Baal and Mot, *CTA* 6) is uncertain, the scribe is named along with what is probably the name of the chief priest (whose titles are given) as well as the name of the king. The mention of the chief priest suggests a link with the cult, and the very presence of the colophon may imply that the text was specially inscribed. There are also indications that the texts were not merely intended to be left in the library, for they contain what appear to be directions to someone who is reading aloud. The relevant words are,

wtb lmspr ktlàkn ġlmm
And recite again: 'When the servants were sent...' (*CTA* 4 v 104f).

(The words have been ruled off by the scribe.)
And,

whnd/bt ytb lmspr

And this (?)/'And behold a house...' he shall recite again (*CTA* 19 E).

(An instruction to read again the passage alongside which the words are written, or else to return to a particular phrase.)

In the Shaḥar and Shalim text there is apparently an instruction to repeat a certain passage five times, but the text is broken, before a reference to an assembly (*CTA* 23 56–7). In view of these passages we are presumably to think of a reading aloud of the texts, though whether this recital would be accompanied by some form of dramatic ritual, or whether the texts actually represent the words spoken by those who were enacting the drama is uncertain.

A further piece of evidence for a close connection between the texts and the cult is provided by one of the texts, namely that which contains the story of the birth of the gods Shaḥar and Shalim. On this single tablet is found not only the account of the birth of various gods, but a number of brief passages some of which have the appearance of mythological extracts, while others seem to be instructions for various rituals. What connection, if any, exists between the ritual instructions and the mythological passages is unclear, but their presence on the same tablet suggests a link between literary and cultic activity. We must also remember the possibility that the accounts of the activities of the gods were preserved in oral as well as written form by the priests; indeed, it has often been argued that the texts may have reached their advanced style thanks to the 'polishing' they received at the oral stage.

It has been necessary to engage in this discussion, because the answer to the question whether anything is known of the religious festivals of Ugarit depends very much on how far the texts are cultic and reflect ritual events. While we must be wary of the danger of the circular argument, there is a *prima facie* case for suggesting that since there does seem to be evidence for a connection between the texts and the cult then the contents of the texts must reflect something of the nature of the festivals in which they were used. A similar debate has taken place concerning the so-called Enthronement Psalms in the Old Testament, on the basis of which attempts have been made to reconstruct an autumnal New Year Festival whose central feature was a celebration of Yahweh's enthronement as king. An analogy has been seen in the Babylonian *akitu* or New Year Festival, wherein the great deeds of Marduk, the patron deity of Babylon, as recorded in the tablets of the creation epic *Enuma Elish*, were recounted and enacted, culminating in the celebration of his supremacy over the other gods and the building of a temple in his honour.

In view of the contents of the Baal texts it has been argued that the major cultic festival of ancient Ugarit must have been just such an autumnal New Year Festival. Baal, it must be remembered, was a god of rain and storm and thus the bestower of fertility to the soil in a land whose fertility depended not on the annual inundations of the great rivers, as in Egypt and Mesopotamia, but on the coming of the rains at the correct time and in the correct measure. Thus the time when the autumnal rains were beginning would be the appropriate occasion for celebrating Baal's victories over his rivals Yam and Mot and the building of a temple to set the seal on his kingship. His victory over Yam, the personification of the waters, proved that Baal could check the potential threat which the waters posed. His periodic victories over Mot, who represented death and sterility, proved that despite times when the earth appeared arid and infertile, Baal would return to restore fertility. And if we are correct to believe that these victories were recounted or enacted in the cult, it is possible that we should envisage the worshippers participating by weeping and lamenting or by rejoicing at the appropriate points in the ceremony. It is also likely that we should think of such a festival as more than a mere recalling of Baal's victories; rather, the intention may have been creative – the actualising of the victories in the cult would in some way help to ensure the victories, and therefore that the lifegiving rains would return in due season and in due measure.

Before concluding this discussion on the relationship between the texts and the cult, we should mention that several specific passages in the texts have been thought to reflect particular rituals. Notably it is argued that some ritual must underly the description of Anat's treatment of the body of Mot (*CTA* 6 ii 30ff.). The story of the attempt to place Athtar on Baal's throne in the latter's absence (which immediately precedes the passage just mentioned) has been thought to reflect some ceremony wherein a substitute king was enthroned. The Shaḥar and Shalim text which, as we have seen, includes what appear to be several ritual instructions, has been associated with a cultic feast and perhaps a *hieros gammos* (sacred marriage). However, it must be stressed that it is difficult to speak with any certainty about the precise nature of the religious festivals of Ugarit.

It has been noted already that the people of Ugarit constructed elaborate tombs for their deceased, and that their construction included facilities for the provision of refreshment for the dead. This raises the question of how death and the underworld were understood, and whether there was any belief in some form of worthwhile *post-mortem* existence. To attempt to answer this question it may be useful to look at the Ugaritic texts for information.

A number of passages in the story of Aqhat are instructive in this context. Death was regarded as the departure of the *npš*, usually translated 'soul' (so Driver) or 'breath' (so Gibson) (*CTA* 18 iv 24,36;19 ii 87?, 91-2?); such a view is reminiscent of many statements in the Old Testament where death is described as the departure or taking away of the *nepeš* (cf. e.g. Gen. 35:18; Jud. 16:30; 1Ki. 17:21; Job 11:20; 31:39; Jer.15:9 Jonah 4:3). That death was seen as the common lot of all mankind is suggested by some words addressed to Anat by Aqhat,

> What does a man get as a fate?
> What does a man get as a final lot?
> Glaze will be poured on (my) head,
> Quicklime on the top of my crown,
> And the death of all I shall die,
> And I myself shall indeed die.   (*CTA* 17 vi 35ff.; cf. Ps.49:10-12)

It should be noted that these words are a response to Anat's offer to grant Aqhat immortality in return for his marvellous bow which she coveted. This might suggest that it was thought to be the prerogative of the gods to bestow immortality if they so wished. However, Aqhat proceeds to accuse the goddess of lying, and utters the above words on the fate of mankind. The implication is that death was believed to be the fate shared by mortals, though, as we have seen, there is some evidence that the kings of Ugarit were accorded some sort of divine status after death. The incident in the story of Keret wherein Sha'taqat heals the ailing Keret and which culminates in the statement,

Death was truly shattered,

Sha'taqat was truly victorious (*CTA* 16 vi 13-14)

must be seen as an instance of cheating death; Keret was as good as dead but not actually dead.

Near the beginning of tablet 17, where Baal intercedes with El on behalf of Daniel who has no son, there is a section which lists the duties of a son (*CTA* 17 i 27ff.). Although the precise significance of some of the terminology is far from certain, it is reasonably clear that these duties include the performing of various funerary rites, perhaps involving the setting up of some form of memorial or stele of the ancestral gods (cf.2 Sam.18:18). Doubtless the necessity that the correct funerary rights should be performed provides one of the major reasons for the stress on the importance of leaving behind progeny in the stories of Aqhat and Keret. In this context, it should be noted that the will of Arḥalbu (already mentioned), in which it is stipulated that his widow shall marry his brother, has been cited as a parallel to the Israelite practice of levirate marriage, which underlines the importance of leaving offspring (cf. Dt.25:5-6; Mt.22:24; Mk.12:19; Lk.20:28). Here however, it would be dangerous to assume that this text suggests that this was the normal practice at Ugarit; not only is it impossible to know what special circumstances may have called for the stipulation, but the very fact that it was made suggests that the widow would not have married her brother-in-law as a matter of course.

To the people of Ugarit, the lord of death was Mot, the voracious god of the underworld who engaged in periodic combat with Baal. His abode was subterranean, and the dead are described as 'those who go down into the earth' (*rdm àrṣ*). Mot is described as being

. . .within his city 'Miry';

a pit is the throne on which he sits,

filth is the land of his inheritance.   (*CTA* 4 viii 11-14; 5 ii 15-17)

The notion of the underworld being a muddy place is not uncommon, and is found, for example, in Greek and Mesopotamian thought; a similar idea is probably to be found in Pss. 40:2 and 69:14-15 (cf. v.2) where the reference to 'the pit' suggests that the Psalmists' distress is envisaged in terms of being overwhelmed by the mud and waters of the underworld. In a passage which describes Mot's great appetite (*CTA* 5 i 14ff.) there is a reference to the fact that he eats mud (*ḥmr*), which may again reflect the nature of his abode, though Gibson renders the word 'clay' and, in a footnote to his translation, suggests that it here signifies the bodies of men. If Gibson is correct, the passage provides evidence for a belief that the dead were devoured by Mot, and this seems to be the implication of the first words that are legible in the second column of tablet *CTA* 5. Mot is apparently being described,

(A lip to?) the earth, a lip to the heavens
(?) a tongue (?) to the stars.
Baal shall enter his inside,
into his mouth he shall descend.

It seems that the notion of the underworld swallowing up the dead is expressed in terms of the deity of the underworld devouring them (cf. also *CTA* 4 viii 18-19; 6 ii 22-23).

The fact that in some Old Testament passages (Ps.88:10; Prov.9:18; Is.14:9; 26:14), the Hebrew term *rᵉpā'îm* refers to the dead, and that in the Phoenician Eshmun'azar and Tabnit inscriptions *rp'm* also refers to the dead, could lead to the conclusion that references to the *rpùm* in the Ugarit texts are to be understood as allusions to the dead as well. The Ugaritic term has been rendered 'shades' by e.g. Gordon and Driver. But whether the term must be so understood is far from clear. We have noted that in texts *CTA* 20, 21 and 22, in so far as their contents can be reconstructed, we see the *rpùm* attending a banquet having travelled via threshing floors and plantations (a fact which has led to the suggestion that they were associated with fertility), riding on chariots and asses. In these texts, the word *rpùm* is sometimes paralleled by the term *ilnym*, usually understood to mean 'deities', suggesting that they perhaps had divine status. Another passage in which the *rpùm* are called *ilnym* is *CTA* 6 vi 44ff. where they are associated with the sun goddess Shapash; here they are also called or linked with *ilm* ('gods') and *mtm* (perhaps 'the dead' but the word might also mean 'men'). A further complication arises from the wish, expressed in the Keret story, that Keret may be exalted,

btk rpi àrṣ   in the midst of the *rpùm* of the earth/underworld,
bpḫr qbṣ dtn   in the assembly of the gathering of *dtn*
(*CTA* 15 iii 3-4,14-15)

Since *dtn* appears to be a tribal name, and since Keret is alive, the suggestion might be that the *rpùm* were not the dead, unless àrṣ here, as in some other passages, has the sense 'underworld', and the hope is being expressed that he will join the *rpùm* in the future. A recently published text (RS 34.126) preserves a ritual in which the well-being of Ugarit is sought in the name of king 'Ammurapi; various individuals and groups are invoked including Ammistamru, Niqmaddu, the *rpi àrṣ* ('*rpùm* of the earth/underworld'), the *qbṣ ddn* (presumably the same as *qbṣ dtn*, 'gathering of *dtn*', mentioned above), and the *rpim qdmym*, 'the ancient *rpùm*'.

In view of the variety of these references, it would be dangerous to conclude that all are simply references to the dead, and that, for example, the dead were thought to attend a heavenly banquet. The last mentioned text suggests that the *rpùm* were perhaps the ancient ancestors; the fact that these are apparently the king's ancestors could perhaps be linked with the evidence already noted that the kings may have been thought to become divine after death to account for the fact that the *rpùm* are called gods, and share in El's banquet. It might also be argued that, in the Keret story, the hope is being expressed that king Keret may, in due time, be exalted among that company. But any such suggestion can only be advanced with the utmost caution, and it is perhaps unwise to assume that the term has precisely the same signification in each occurrence. In a detailed study of the relevant material (*Rank among the Canaanite Gods: El, Ba'al, and the Repha'im*, Harvard Semitic Monographs 21, Missoula, 1979) C.E. L'Heureux has suggested that we should distinguish three categories; (a) the *rpi àrṣ* ('*rpùm* of the earth') who are not dead, but rather a living group, perhaps of élite charioteers, (b) the *rpim qdmym* ('*rpùm* of old') who include the royal ancestors, and (c) the *rpùm* who are *ilnym*, 'gods', the heavenly *rpùm* who share El's banquet; the heavenly banquet is the counterpart of the feast of the earthly *rpùm*, and, he suggests, the extension of a term which referred to a living group to apply to certain dead persons represents the latest development in the term's use.

That there was an individual deity referred to as *rpù* seems to be confirmed by text RS 24.252, wherein *rpù*, described as 'eternal king' (*mlk 'lm*), drinks in company with other deities, while music is played. There has been considerable debate as to whether *rpù* is to be identified with one of the major deities, e.g. El or (perhaps less likely) Baal, or whether he is to be regarded as a distinct deity. This is uncertain, as is the precise connection between the individual *rpù* and the *rpùm*, but it is possible that he was their patron deity. Daniel is frequently described as *mt rpi* ('man of *rpù*'), suggesting a close relationship with this deity.

Further Reading

I. Engnell, *Studies in Divine Kingship in the Ancient Near East*, 2nd. edition, Oxford, 1967.

J. Gray, 'Sacral Kingship in Ugarit', *Ugaritica* VI (*MRS* XVII), Paris, 1969.

J. Gray, *Near Eastern Mythology*, London, 1969.

A.S. Kapelrud, *Baal in the Ras Shamra Texts*, Copenhagen, 1952.

J.C. de Moor, 'The Semitic Pantheon of Ugarit', *UF* II, 1970.

J.C. de Moor, *The Seasonal Pattern in the Ugaritic Myth of Ba'lu according to the Version of Ilimilku*, Neukirchen-Vluyn, 1971.

U. Oldenburg, *The Conflict between El and Baal in Canaanite Religion*, Leiden, 1965.

M.H. Pope, *El in the Ugaritic Texts* (*Supplements to VT* II), Leiden, 1955.

P.J. van Zijl, *Baal: a study of texts in connection with Baal in the Ugaritic epics*, Neukirchen-Vluyn, 1972.

6

Ugarit and the Bible

It is abundantly clear that Ugarit was an important city of ancient Syria. But what is the justification for including a volume on this city in a series *Cities of the Biblical World*? Is is merely that the discovery of Ugarit has increased our knowledge of the ancient Near East – the general context from which the Bible arose, or even that the texts unearthed there shed light on the nature of the god Baal to whom such frequent reference is made in certain Old Testament passages? The answer must be that the significance is much greater, despite the fact that, as indicated in the Introduction, there can have been no direct influence of the Ugaritic literature upon ancient Israel. In so far as Ugarit may be regarded as representative of Canaanite thought, the texts are not simply relevant for our understanding of Canaanite religion, but they help us to assess the extent to which the Hebrews borrowed and adapted Canaanite ideas. Moreover, the discovery of a hitherto unknown Semitic language which proved to be closely akin to Hebrew has not merely increased our knowledge of North West Semitic, but has helped to elucidate aspects of the Hebrew of the Old Testament, and provide a wider context in which to study problematic vocabulary.

In a volume such as this, it is possible only to attempt to illustrate briefly some of the features of the Hebrew language for which Ugaritic may have relevance. Perhaps the second verse of the Bible is a suitable starting point.

> The earth was without form and void, with darkness over the face of the abyss, and a mighty wind that swept over the surface of the waters (*or* and the spirit of God hovering over the surface of the waters).

The use of the verb *rḥp* in the story of Aqhat to refer to the activity of eagles (*nšrm*) soaring or hovering above the ground, supports the view that the participial form (*m^eraḥepet*) describes the 'spirit of God' (*rûᵃḥ ᵉlōhîm*) as 'hovering' over the waters (so N.E.B. margin; cf. Deut. 32:11 where N.E.B. translates the verb 'hovers') rather than merely 'moving' (so A.V., R.S.V.) or 'brooding' (R.V.), and reduces the likelihood that the subject is a 'mighty wind' (N.E.B.).

The fact that Ugaritic *ṯpṭ*, 'judge', regularly parallels *zbl*, 'prince', in references to the god Yam/Nahar, lends support to the belief that Hebrew *šōpēṭ* can bear a wider connotation than 'one who administers justice' – a description hardly adequate for the charismatic tribal leaders traditionally known as the 'Judges'.

The usage in Ugaritic of *l* to introduce a vocative may help to account for certain apparently awkward or unnecessary usages of *l[e]* in the Old Testament, where resort to emendation was the usual solution. A literal translation of Psalm 73:1 yields the awkward, 'Truly good to Israel (is) God to those who are pure in heart.' Most recent translations and commentators have overcome the problem by assuming that the consonants *lyśr'l* (to Israel) should be divided *lyśr/'l* (to the upright/God). This could lead to a rendering, 'Truly good to the upright is God, is God to those who are pure in heart' (though the double reference to God which such an emendation seems to require is frequently overlooked in translations). In his commentary on the Psalter, M. Dahood suggests that we should understand *lyśr'l* as 'O Israel', and renders the verse, 'Truly good, O Israel, is God to the pure in heart.'

A word of caution should be introduced here, particularly over the use of Ugaritic to establish supposed new etymologies for Hebrew words, sometimes on the assumption that homonyms have not been recognised. J. Barr has drawn attention to the inherent dangers in his *Comparative Philology and the Text of the Old Testament.* The obvious point needs to be stressed that although Ugaritic and Hebrew are akin they are not identical.

An area of Hebrew study to which the Ugaritic literature has been thought to be particularly relevant is that of poetry. The fact that both Ugaritic and Hebrew poetry have as their most striking feature *parallelismus membrorum*, i.e. the same or similar sense is given twice (or occasionally three times) in different words, and that 'fixed pairs' of parallel terms (e.g. sea/river, hand/right hand, heart/liver) are common to both languages, suggest that they shared a common poetic tradition, though it should be noted that they are not alone in exhibiting parallelism. It has even been suggested that Psalm 29 was of Canaanite origin and was a hymn in praise of Baal as lord of the thunder; subsequently the psalm was adapted for Israelite use by the substitution of 'Yahweh' for 'Baal'. This understanding of the psalm has not been universally accepted by any means, but many scholars have noted its Canaanite affinities.

The presence in Ugaritic poetry of instances wherein two verbs in a sequence employ the 'perfect' (*qtl*) form and a third verb employs the 'imperfect' (*yqtl*) form, may cause the Old Testament scholar to pause before emending passages of Hebrew poetry which exhibit a similar phenomenon apparently in contravention of usual narrative principles. The Ugaritic poems have been employed in discussions of whether 'metre' in ancient Semitic poetry is based on the number of stressed syllables in a line, or on the number of syllables irrespective of stress; however, the uncertainty as to precisely how the Ugaritic language was pronounced places limits on its value in helping to solve this particular problem.

Hitherto we have been speaking in rather general terms but there are a number of items of religious vocabulary – particular words and phrases – which may be elucidated by reference to the Ugaritic literature. Most notable among these is the designation of Yahweh in Psalm 68:4 as 'he who rides upon the clouds' (*rōkēb bāʿarābôt*), since a frequent epithet of Baal in the Ugaritic texts is 'he who rides the clouds' (*rkb ʿrpt*). There has been discussion over the precise significance of the Hebrew and Ugaritic terms, and it has been suggested that the Hebrew epithet perhaps means 'he who rides in the deserts'. However, it seems likely that the picture we are to imagine is that of the bringer of rain and storm riding upon the clouds which form his chariot (cf. Ps.104:3b and perhaps 65:11). It is probable that an epithet of Baal has here been attributed to Yahweh.

English versions have been content to translate Psalm 48:2 as though it describes Mount Zion as being in the north (A.V. 'on the sides of the north'; R.S.V. 'in the north'; J.B. 'deep heart of the north'; N.E.B. 'like the farthest reaches of the north') despite the geographical problem this poses unless we are to posit some extreme southerly location for the psalmist when he composed this description of the holy mountain! The Hebrew for 'north', *Ṣāpôn*, was derived from the mountain in the north which, the Ugaritic texts make it clear, was believed by the people of Ugarit to have been the abode of Baal, i.e. *ṣpn* (Mons Casius, Jebel Aqra). Rather than being located in the north, Zion is here being likened to the abode of Baal, Mount *Ṣapan* (cf. N.E.B. margin).

The personification of the forces of death and sterility, in particular in the form of the god Mot (*mt*), to which the Ugaritic texts bear witness, may well provide the background for the understanding of Old Testament passages wherein death (*māwet*) is personified. In Psalm 49:14 death is described as the shepherd of those who descend to Sheol (so most modern translators and commentators – A.V. 'death shall feed on them'). The likening of the dead here to sheep is reminiscent of passages in the Ugaritic texts which speak of Mot making the dead 'like a lamb in his mouth ... like a kid in the opening of his windpipe' (*CTA* 4 viii 18–19; 6 ii 22–23). Such passages raise the possibility that in Psalm 44:11,22 the phrase 'like sheep for the slaughter' is employing a word picture wherein it is death who slaughters the 'sheep'. The notion of the dead being devoured is seen in Isaiah 5:14 where it is Sheol, the abode of the dead, which is described as opening its throat to receive the dead (cf. Num. 16:30; Ps. 141:7; Prov. 1:12; Hab. 2:5). Another simile employed in the Old Testament to describe death, wherein death is personified, is that of the hunter laying snares and traps (2 Sam. 22:6; Pss. 18:5; 116:3; Prov. 13:14; 14:27).

There is, in general, a great deal of similarity between Ugaritic and Hebrew views on death and the nature of the underworld. This is probably to be explained as due to a common Semitic background rather than Hebrew adaptation of Canaanite ideas. Attention has been drawn to a number of other possible Old Testament parallels in the course of our outline of Ugaritic beliefs about death and the abode of Mot, but one or two further points deserve special mention here. The fact that in Ugaritic *árṣ*, 'earth', sometimes refers to the underworld may support the belief that Hebrew *'ereṣ* can sometimes have this particular sense (cf. e.g. Ex.15:12; 1 Sam.28:13; Job 10:21; Pss.7:5(?); 63:9; 71:20; 95:4(?); 106:17; 141:7 (? – but note the parallel 'Sheol');143:3; Is.26:19; 29:4; Jer.15:7(?); Ezek.31:14; Jonah 2:6).

On analogy with the passage in the story of Aqhat, already noted (p.103f) wherein Anat invites Aqhat to ask for life (*ḥym*) in return for his marvellous bow, M.Dahood has suggested, in his commentary on the Psalms and elsewhere, that Hebrew *ḥayyîm* can sometimes have the sense 'eternal life'; further, since he believes there to be clear evidence from Ugarit of a belief in resurrection and immortality, he has argued that there is no necessity to think that the Israelites only had such ideas at a late date. In the third volume of this commentary on the Psalms (pp.xliiiff.) he has gathered together evidence which he has found throughout the Psalter and elsewhere in the Old Testament for a Hebrew belief in resurrection and immortality and an 'Elysian Fields' motif; various words and word-pictures have been re-interpreted in the light of this proposed concept – interpretations which, Dahood argues, have been thought impossible because of a preconception among other scholars that such ideas must be late.

Dahood's views on this subject have not generally commended themselves. The Ugaritic evidence for such beliefs is at best uncertain and perhaps, as we suggested earlier, contrary. In any case, even if it could be proved true for Ugarit, it would be unwise to assume that *all* aspects of Ugaritic and Hebrew beliefs about death were similar. If Dahood's interpretations are correct, it is difficult to see how or when the 'correct' understanding came to be lost. Nor is it easy to understand why there should be so much stress on the leaving behind of descendants who will perpetuate the 'name' and memory of the deceased, and why we find hopes for and promises of long life rather than eternal life, if the latter were really thought possible. It is strange that no clear references to such a belief are to be found in the prophetical books (with the exception of Is.26:19, which is widely held to be late) where it might reasonably be expected in contexts of Yahweh's punishment and judgement of his people; even more strange is the lack of reference to such a belief in the Book of Job if there were believed to be an afterlife wherein the righteous could be rewarded. It seems far more likely that throughout the greater part of the Old Testament period there was no belief in a worthwile afterlife; apart from one or two special individuals such as Enoch and Elijah (Gen.5:24; 2 Ki. 2:11), the Israelites could expect only a shady existence in Sheol. There are, however, hints at the emergence of a more positive belief in Is.26:19, already mentioned, and Dan. 12:2, thought by the majority of scholars to date from the second century BC.

In view of the complicated nature of the references to the *rpùm* in the Ugaritic texts, it is difficult to asses the extent to which they can shed light on references to the *rᵉpā'îm* in the Old Testament. We have mentioned (p.105) that in some Old Testament passages the term refers to the dead. However, elsewhere the word designates an extinct people who formerly dwelt in the area of Palestine and who appear to have been characterized by exceptional size (Gen. 14:5; Dt.2:10f.; 3:11; Josh.17:15 cf. 2 Sam.21:16,20). Both strands in the Old Testament tradition can perhaps be paralleled in the Ugaritic material. Ugaritic passages wherein the *rpùm* appear to be dead, notably the dead royal ancestors, can be related to Old Testament passages wherein the *rᵉpā'îm* are the dead; particularly noteworthy is Is.14:9, where the term seems to refer to dead rulers. The use of Hebrew *rᵉpā'im* to refer to pre-Israelite inhabitants of the land could be regarded as simply an extension of the same basic idea; the dead were those who lived many years ago, thence the earlier occupants of the land. However, in the Old Testament the two usages do seem to be distinct, so it might be argued that we should look rather to Ugaritic passages which have been interpreted as referring to a military élite; this would be especially appropriate in relation to the reference to warriors described as descendants of the 'giants' (*hārāpāh* – 2 Sam.21:16,20), and to Og, king of Bashan (Dt.3:11). It has been suggested that Og's enigmatic 'bedstead' might have been a group of dolmens (cf. C. Rabin, 'Og', *Eretz-Israel* VIII, 1967, pp.75*–76* [English summary], 251–4 [article in Hebrew]), and associations between megaliths and earlier inhabitants of the land may have something to do with traditions about their greater stature.

It is possible, therefore, that the two distinct Old Testament traditions about the *rᵉpā'îm* are to be related to earlier traditions, and that the Ugaritic literature can be of relevance in elucidating the background. Nevertheless, it is appropriate to add a note of caution, and beware of the assumption that the Ugaritic and Hebrew terms must have had precisely the same significance.

Numerous other instances could be cited where similarities or close parallels have been noted between Ugaritic and Hebrew terms and phrases, and where, at the very least, it is true to say that the discovery of the Ugaritic literature has been of relevance in that it must now be borne in mind in any discussion of the Hebrew terms. Two more examples must suffice. Considerations of the concept of the divine assembly in Israelite thought must take into account the fact that Psalm 82:1 employs a term, *ʿadat ʾēl* (literally 'assembly of God/El'), used of the divine assembly in the Ugaritic texts (*ʿdt ilm*, 'assembly of the gods/El'). Similarly, Old Testament reference to the divine beings as *bᵉnê ʾēlîm* literally 'sons of gods; cf. for example (Ps. 29:1; 89:6) recall the Ugaritic phrase *bn ilm* 'gods/sons of El'. Those who, in Ugaritic thought, are deities in their own right are, in Hebrew tradition, members of Yahweh's assembly, called upon to praise him, but not comparable to him. Are we to see here a reflection of the process whereby Yahweh was elevated to the rank of king above all gods, and the other gods are denigrated until they become mere lackeys?

What relevance has the employment of 'bull' terminology in the Ugaritic texts to describe Baal, Mot and especially El, whose stock epithet is *tr* 'the bull', to our understanding of Old Testament passages which record the making of bull/calf images (Ex. 32; 1 Ki. 12:28ff.)? It is impossible here to discuss the many problems which underlie the question of the historicity of the story of Aaron's calf, and in particular whether it represents a much later attempt to put back into the Mosaic period a condemnation of the making of such images. That Jeroboam had such images made when he set up sanctuaries for his northern kingdom in Dan and Bethel is not seriously questioned. It does not seem likely that Jeroboam would have introduced a pagan cult into his sanctuaries. It has been suggested, on the basis of certain ancient Near Eastern analogies, that the bulls were regarded as pedestals of Yahweh, rather than images of him. However, it is difficult to see how mere pedestals would cause such anger and condemnation as were aroused by the construction of the bulls. It must also be noted that 1 Kings 12:28 records the words of Jeroboam to the people thus, 'You have gone up to Jerusalem long enough. *Behold your gods*, O Israel, who brought you up out of the land of Egypt.' If, then, these were images of Yahweh, is it possible to find an explanation for Jeroboam's decision so to represent him?

It is noteworthy that one of the images was set up at Bethel, a sanctuary with which the Jacob traditions seem to have been particularly associated, and where, according to those traditions, Jacob's God revealed himself (Gen. 28:10ff.). Although the biblical account suggests that the name Bethel arose from Jacob's experience that the place was the 'house of God', it is more likely that the story contains an aetiological element, and that the name was originally derived from a temple of El in that location. If this is so, the story reflects an ancestor of Israel taking as his particular guardian the deity of Bethel, i.e. El, who is described in the Ugaritic texts as 'the bull'. The bull image could, then, be part of Israel's sacred past if the forefathers worshipped El. We shall mention later the widely held view that Yahweh and El were at some stage assimilated. Here, it should be noted that if the previous suggestion is correct, it would lend support to the view that *'ābîr yaʿᵃqōb*, usually rendered 'Mighty One of Jacob', should be interpreted as 'Bull of Jacob' (cf. Ugaritic *ibr* 'bull', and Hebrew *'abbîr(îm)* which seems to refer to bull(s) in Pss. 22:13(M.T.); 50:13; 68:31(M.T.); and probably Is. 10:13; 34:7).

Our illustrations have begun to take us from discussion of specific words and phrases to the realm of more general concepts. While it is not surprising that much emphasis has been placed on these individual words and phrases, it is perhaps in the more nebulous area of religious ideas that the Ugaritic texts have their greatest relevance for Biblical study. This relevance can appear in what may at first sight seem unlikely places. For example, J.A. Emerton has argued cogently that Canaanite mythology may provide the background to the imagery of Daniel 7 ('The origin of the Son of Man imagery,' *JTS* NS IX, 1958, pp.225ff.). Evidence from the Ugaritic texts on the significance of temple building as setting the seal on a claim to kingship among the gods may be relevant to the understanding of the importance of the Jerusalem temple and its festivals celebrating the kingship of Yahweh. Indeed, the Ugaritic texts shed considerable light on the whole notion of the kingship of the gods.

We have already noted that the likelihood that an epithet of Baal, 'he who rides the clouds', has been appropriated for Yahweh. This epithet belongs to the realm of the bestowing of fertility to the earth, and it is perhaps within this area of their activities, and the closely related area of the subjugation of the waters, that similarities between Baal and Yahweh are most striking. In Ugarit, where the farmers were dependent on the rains for their livelihood, the giver of fertility was the deity in whose control were the rains and the storms. This control did not only involve the sending of the rain, for this might in fact be a menace if the rains exceeded the desirable limits; thus the giver of fertility was he who had averted the threat of chaos which the waters might produce if not kept in check. For the people of Ugarit, the deity who performed these functions was Baal, whose portraits, as we have noted, depict him armed with club and thunderbolt – the attributes of the sender of the storm.

When we turn to the Old Testament, it is clear that it is Yahweh who bestows fertility. Indeed, an important difference between the fertility bestowing powers of Baal and Yahweh is that the latter's powers are not subject

114

to the interference of other forces so do not suffer periodic fluctuations, as do Baal's at the hands of Mot; Yahweh can by his own decision withhold as well as bestow fertility. But in other respects their activities in this realm are strikingly similar. For example, in Psalm 74:13ff. we find the themes of the sending of fertility to the earth, and the ordering of times and seasons, associated with a victory over the waters, personified in the form of monsters. Within this passage, the mention of the crushing of the heads of Leviathan is significant, for this monster can hardly be other than *ltn*, 'the twisting serpent, the tyrant with seven heads' slain by Baal according to *CTA* 5 i 1ff. (We should however note that in *CTA* 3 iii 36ff. Anat claims to have slain a number of monsters, including Yam and 'the twisting serpent, the tyrant with seven heads', which is presumably *ltn*, though the name does not appear in this passage.) Thus Yahweh is credited with having performed a feat ascribed to Baal in the Ugaritic literature (cf. Is.27:1).

The other reference to Leviathan in the Psalter (Ps. 104:26) presents a different picture; here Leviathan is one of Yahweh's creatures, a mere plaything, yet earlier in the psalm (vv.5–9) there has been a declaration of Yahweh's control over the seas, and the establishment of bounds which the waters must not pass. We have attempted to demonstrate elsewhere ('The "Subjugation of the Waters" Motif in the Psalms; Imagery or Polemic?' *JSS* XXIII, 1978, pp.245ff.) the prominence of the theme of the subjugation of the waters in the psalms, where we find, in addition to statements of actual conflict with personifications of the waters (Ps. 89:9–10; cf. Is. 51:9–10), passages where the waters are called upon to praise Yahweh (Ps. 96:11; 98:7–8), and where Yahweh is enthroned above or dominant over the waters (Pss. 29:3,10; 65:7; 93:3–4). Particular mention should be made of some passages where the events associated with the Exodus are expressed in terms reminiscent of the subjugation of the waters. The most graphic is in the closing verses of Psalm 77 where Yahweh's intervention in the history of his people is expressed in terms of the cosmic theophany of the storm god. Such a description is strikingly reminiscent of the great mythological battles of the storm god against the sea monster. Other references to this demonstration in his people's history of Yahweh's power to 'divide the sea' are to be found in Isaiah 51:9–10; Psalms 66:5–7; 106:9; 114:1–5; 136:13. The significance of such passages will be discussed shortly, but perhaps the clue is to be found in Psalm 74 where we began this part of our discussion. Several times in the psalm there are references to the scoffing of the enemy; the psalmist is seeking to answer those who claim that Yahweh is powerless.

The relevance of the Ugaritic material for the study of the Bible goes far beyond the provision of important background material. It also goes beyond the furnishing of valuable evidence of religious terminology, and of a language whose vocabulary, grammar and syntax may help our interpretation of problematical Hebrew passages. These aspects are of immense importance, but when the material is related specifically to statements about Yahweh in a certain passage of the Old Testament, we find ourselves facing something far more fundamental, namely the process by which Yahweh came to be the complex deity whose various facets are praised in the Hebrew psalms and other Old Testament passages.

It is to be regretted, though perhaps expected, that Ugaritic has thrown no light on the vexed question of the absolute origins of the cult of Yahweh. However, it is probably true to say that the material is relevant to a relatively early period in the development of Yahwism, and that we should perhaps even think of a period before the ancestors of Israel came into contact with the cult of Yahweh, i.e. in the Patriarchal period. The writing of the Ugaritic texts can be dated with some accuracy to the period c.1400–1350 BC, i.e. within two centuries, and perhaps not much more than a century, of the most widely accepted date for the Exodus. It therefore seems probable that they reflect beliefs which would continue to be held among some Canaanites at least at the time when Israelites were settling in the Promised Land. It is equally probable that the texts as we have them represent the result of a tradition which had been growing for many years, in which case they reflect beliefs current at a time when forefathers of elements which later made up Israel were already in the land of Canaan.

Many scholars have suggested that, at an early stage, Yahweh and the Canaanite El had become equated, an important reason for this assumption being that there seems to have been no tension between the cults of El and Yahweh such as existed between those of Baal and Yahweh. Indeed, the difference in attitude to the use of the divine name 'ēl from that exhibited towards ba'al in the Old Testament is most striking. It is difficult to be certain at what point this assimilation took place, and we should be wary of assuming that the process can be associated with any one period. It does not seem improbable that the Patriarchs, as leaders of groups taking part in tribal migrations, would have tribal gods who would be characterised by their association with a group of people rather than a locality, and by a relationship to the worshipper to be envisaged in terms of kinship. As we have seen, stories such as that of the revelation to Jacob at Bethel may reflect a process of identification of the Patriarchal gods with El (the bull El becomes the bull-god of Jacob), when contact was made with his cult in Canaan. Thus, the tribal gods, being identified with various manifestations of El, merged into a 'God of the Fathers' who was, in fact, El. That this identification could take place without engendering any such tension as existed between Yahweh and Baal may imply that the characteristics involved were such as would facilitate, or at least not militate against, the process. After the Exodus the God of the Fathers/El was identified with Yahweh – a process which the theologising of the later biblical writers has reversed by suggesting that the ancestors of Israel, without realising, were really worshipping Yahweh whom they knew as El or the God of the Fathers. But other periods may have had a profound effect on the assimilation, for example in the bringing to Jerusalem, the cult centre of El Elyon, of the Ark of the Covenant, and the making of this Jebusite sanctuary the focus of Yahwism.

If at a relatively early stage of the development of Yahwism El and Yahweh had become assimilated, we should expect the majority of El's attributes to be the same as attributes of Yahweh. Thanks to the Ugaritic texts we can be much clearer as to what the attributes of El were. There are, of course, aspects of El which are not paralleled in respect of Yahweh. El appears as a figure of seniority among the gods, whose power is being challenged but is nevertheless still real. This must be seen in the context of the changing situation at Ugarit wherein El was gradually supplanted and lost his dominant position. It is likely that Yahweh's identification with El would lead to an association of El's consort with Yahweh, and that this would continue to be a feature of popular piety. But it is not surprising that there is no explicit evidence in the Old Testament that Yahweh was thought to have a consort, and that if such beliefs existed they were eventually suppressed. The various references to Asherah(s) (Athirat) in the Old Testament seem to be to a foreign deity, or an image or symbol of the deity whose cult was considered an abomination by the Old Testament writers. El appears in the Ugaritic texts as the 'bull' and as the father of the gods. It is not impossible that the presence of the bull image in Hebrew tradition may be linked with the identification of Yahweh and El, nor is it impossible that Old Testament references to the 'sons of God/the gods' owe something to the notion of a father of the gods, though the terms may be analogous to such phrases as 'sons of the prophets' and 'sons of strength' (i.e. 'men of valour') and not imply any physical relationship. However, it is not impossible that the presence around Yahweh of a heavenly court may have originated from his identification with El. We recall the use of the phrase '^{a}_dat_ 'ēl in Psalm 82:1, which parallels the Ugaritic '_dt ilm_ 'assembly of El/the gods'.

Since it is impossible to be at all certain what was Yahweh's original nature, it is difficult to assess the extent to which it was modified by assimilation to El. For example, wisdom and holiness may be fundamental attributes of deity, so the fact that El and Yahweh exhibit these characteristics need not imply any borrowing. Contrasts have sometimes been drawn between the so-called benevolence or forbearance of El and a supposed originally martial character of Yahweh. That Yahweh was originally a martial deity is possible, in view of the fact that the tribes rallied in his name at times of mutual threat from external forces; but it could be argued that if it was some form of covenant with Yahweh which was the unifying element behind the tribes prior to the monarchy it would be natural that any attempt to bring about concerted action by several tribes should be made in the name of the God who gave unity. In any case, it is not certain that El was always benevolent.

That an affinity would be seen between the father-god El and the god(s) of the Fathers who stood in a kinship relationship to the worshippers would be natural, so that it is possible that Yahweh adopted the attribute of fatherhood from El/the god(s) of the Fathers. Worshippers of Yahweh continued to think of him as being like a father to his followers. Yahweh stood in a particularly close relationship to the king who was his adopted son and servant; a similar situation is to be seen in Ugarit with reference to Keret, but we should perhaps be wary of treating Keret as merely an earthly monarch. Nevertheless, the Hebrew notion of kingship may have been influenced by the Canaanite; for example, there is some evidence from Ugarit and from Israel that the well-being of the nation was in some way connected with the well-being of the king.

Yahweh may well have appropriated the function of creator of the universe from El, although it must be stressed that no description of creation has yet been found at Ugarit, and the notion that El was creator is inferred from his epithets and from evidence from outside Ugarit. It has also been suggested that the designation of Yahweh as king of the gods is the transfer to him of a designation originally belonging to El. It is important to note that at Ugarit several deities are spoken of in terms of kingship; however, it is El who is enthroned among the gods and receives their homage. We may perhaps say that while El *was* king, Baal *became* a king, so that when we are considering the kingship of Yahweh we must bear in mind the likelihood that the notion was influenced by the thought of Baal's kingship too.

Thanks to his taking over attributes of El, Yahweh had come to be regarded as God from of old, the original creator; he was king, enthroned among the heavenly beings who paid homage. He was holy and wise, and benevolent to those who obeyed and served him. But the Yahweh of whom we read in the Old Testament is far more than this. He was the victorious subduer of the unruly waters who had removed their threat and ordained their limits; he was the sole governor of fertility, and the controller of rain and storm; he was pre-eminent and incomparable, enthroned upon his holy mountain; he was a deity whose saving acts could be seen in the history of his people. With the exception of the last, these are the major attributes of Baal as revealed in the Ugaritic texts; and even the last is sometimes expressed in terms reminiscent of the subduing of the waters.

The similarity is such that we must ask whether we are to think of a conscious likening of Yahweh to Baal, or even a taking over of the functions of the latter for the former, at a time when the two deities confronted each other as their worshippers came into contact. In considering the significance of this similarity we may perhaps begin with the point mentioned at the end of the previous paragraph and ask why the *Heilsgeschichte* ('salvation history') should be expressed in mythological terms. It is argued that in a context of developing religious ideas, primitive mythological notions were gradually demythologised and historicised – the stress on history being a peculiarly Hebrew development. But unless we feel able to discount completely what seems to be one of the most basic truths of Hebrew religion, we must conclude that allegiance to Yahweh was firmly grounded in a historical event, the Exodus. What was believed to be a divine intervention in history lay at the very root of Hebrew devotion to Yahweh, yet it is precisely this event which is sometimes described in terms of a victory over the waters, often personified as a chaos monster. This argues that despite the stress on history, history could be mythologised.

If, in the Hebrew mind, stress was laid upon Yahweh's acts in history so that the Exodus came to assume the role played in Canaanite religious thought by the defeat of the personified-chaos monster, we must ask why mythological terminology should have been used to record it. Are we to think of such mythological allusions merely as imagery, and conclude that in the course of time there was built up a thesaurus of religious descriptive phrases and terminology whose origin lay in poetic statements about Yahweh, bereft of any mythological significance? It may be that we look for something rather deeper, perhaps a conscious stripping of Baal of his attributes and an ascription of these to Yahweh, for mythological descriptions of the *Heilsgeschichte* must be seen in the context of the many statements about Yahweh which are strikingly reminiscent of the attributes of Baal.

In addition to the type of statement just discussed, the whole of Yahweh's powers to bestow fertility and to control the meteorological phenomena of rain and thunder are such as to admit the possibility that Baal's role of bestower of fertility was transferred to Yahweh. Similarly, Yahweh is seen as the establisher of order who has the unruly waters under complete subjection; at times this feature of Yahweh's attributes is expressed in terms of actual conflict in which the waters have been defeated, while at other times we hear of a state of affairs wherein the chaotic waters have been restricted within their limits, and their threat removed. This theme is one which is clearly relevant to the motif of Yahweh's kingship, for this is based upon, amongst other things, the establishment of order. This can be illustrated by a consideration of Psalm 93; here, a declaration of Yahweh's kingship is followed by a statement of the ordering of the earth, and that, despite the noisy threat of the waters, Yahweh is mightier than they; he has thus established a state of rightness in the universe, as he has in society by the establishing of his decrees.

As a result of his demonstration of his power, Yahweh was pre-eminent and incomparable among the other divine beings, as was Baal after his defeat of Yam. Again we must note that whereas we are to see Baal's pre-eminence in a polytheistic context, Yahweh's incomparability is to be seen within the context of an emergent monotheism, wherein other gods have been reduced to the role of mere servants of Yahweh, their king. (There is doubtless a polemic element in such statements.) As king, Yahweh sits enthroned upon his holy mountain. It is probable that Yahweh was associated with a holy mountain from the beginning. The earliest traditions (e.g. Deut. 33:2; Jud. 5:5) suggest that this was originally Sinai, although subsequently Mount Zion became the chosen abode of Yahweh, with the establishment of Jerusalem as his cult centre. But the motif of Baal's enthronement on Mount Ṣapan appears to have coloured Israelite thought about Yahweh's holy mountain, so that the latter may be spoken of in terms of the former. It is not impossible that Hebrew thought on the significance of the building of the temple may have been influenced by Canaanite ideas; the divine king must have a temple to set the seal on his kingship.

We are not, then, merely dealing with a few examples of the *Heilsgeschichte* expressed in mythological terms, but we are facing the fact that Yahweh is credited with Baal's major attributes, and at times in terminology which is such as to make it reasonably clear that this was more than a coincidence. How was it that Baal's characteristics and activities came to be transferred to Yahweh? From the time of Israel's settlement in her own land, certainly down to the time of the fall of Judah, the cults of Baal and Yahweh continued in a state of tension or even conflict, and in the Old Testament there is much polemic against Baal, particularly in the prophetic books. L. Bronner has argued that the Elijah and Elisha stories are to be seen as anti-Baal polemic (*The Stories of Elijah and Elisha as Polemics against Baal Worship*). Condemnation of Baal and the fertility cult was made not simply because Baal was the giver of fertility; this was in itself a useful function, as is shown by the fact that it was stressed for Yahweh. What must be condemned was the suggestion that anyone but Yahweh might bestow fertility, and of course the licentious practices which seem to have accompanied the cult of Baal as fertility god, but which Yahwism could not tolerate. The surest way of combatting the claims of Baal for the affections of the people, and thereby to stamp out the baser practices of the fertility cult, was to assert that

Yahweh, whose worship had no room for immorality, was the sole purveyor of fertility. Further, it had to be claimed that Yahweh could do all that Baal could do for his people – and more, for surely the significance of the conflict of Elijah and the prophets of Baal on Mount Carmel (1 Ki. 18:17ff.) was not so much to test whether or not Baal or Yahweh existed, but which deity was powerful to act on behalf of his people.

Although the Hebrews may have claimed for Yahweh much of what was claimed for the Canaanite Baal, we must not overlook important differences. For example, we do not find any hint in the Old Testament that Yahweh adopted Baal's sexual activity. There are differences within the areas of similarity; Yahweh's establishment of order out of chaos paved the way for the creation of man, unlike Baal's. So Yahweh is not merely a pale reflection of Baal. There seems to be no evidence of the borrowing of the notion of a conflict with Mot, such as we find with reference to the victory over Yam, despite the fact that the similarity between Ugaritic and Hebrew views of death and the underworld is great. Yahweh is no dying/rising god, nor does he have periodic limitations to his powers; indeed, he is able to bring about the opposite to fertility. He is overlord of all which relates to life and death, so there is no room for Baal, no room for Mot, room for no god but Yahweh alone.

Further reference

W.F. Albright, *Yahweh and the Gods of Canaan*, London, 1968.
J. Barr, *Comparative Philology and the Text of the Old Testament*, Oxford, 1968.
L. Bronner, *The Stories of Elijah and Elisha as Polemics against Baal Worship*, Leiden, 1968.
R.J. Clifford, *The Cosmic Mountain in Canaan and the Old Testament* (Harvard Semitic Monographs 4), Cambridge Massachusetts, 1972.
P.C. Craigie, 'The Poetry of Ugarit and Israel', *Tyndale Bulletin* XXII, 1971.
F.M. Cross, *Canaanite Myth and Hebrew Epic: Essays in the History of the Religion of Israel*, Cambridge Massachusetts, 1973.
A.H.W. Curtis, 'The "Subjugation of the Waters" motif in the Psalms; Imagery or Polemic?', *JSS* XXIII, 1978.
M. Dahood, *Psalms* (Anchor Bible), 3 vols., New York, 1965, 1968, 1970.
O. Eissfeldt, 'El and Yahweh', *JSS* I, 1956.
J.A. Emerton, 'The origin of the Son of Man imagery', *JTS* N.S. IX, 1958.
L.R. Fisher, 'Creation at Ugarit and in the Old Testament', *VT* XV, 1965.
L.R. Fisher (ed.), *Ras Shamra Parallels* I, II, III, Rome, 1972, 1975, 1981.

J. Gray, *The Legacy of Canaan: the Ras Shamra Texts and their Relevance to the Old Testament* (*Supplements to VT* V), Leiden, revised edition 1965.

A.S. Kapelrud, *The Ras Shamra Discoveries and the Old Testament*, Oxford, 1965.

P.D. Miller, *The Divine Warrior in Early Israel* (Harvard Semitic Monographs 5), Cambridge Massachusetts, 1973.

M.K. Wakeman, *God's Battle with the Monster: a Study in Biblical Imagery*, Leiden, 1973.

Indexes

General

Aegean 37, 47, 56, 61
Ahat-milki 43, 46, 64
Aistleitner, J. 100
Akkad (ian) 27f, 31, 35f, 60, 88, 99
akitu festival 86, 102
Alabasters (House of) 27, 55
Albanèse, L. 18
Albright, W. F. 26
al Ubaid 35
Amenemhet III 37
Amenophis II 39f, 42
Amenophis III 42f, 88
Amenophis IV (Akhenaten) 44
Ammistamru I 43
Ammistamru II 43, 46
'Ammurapi 43, 47, 106
Amorite(s)/Amurru 35f, 44, 46f, 86
Amosis 39
Anat 66–80, 86, 88, 95, 103, 111, 115
Aqhat 66, 75–8, 96, 99f, 103f, 108, 111
Arhalbu 43, 45, 104
Athirat (Asherah) 67–74, 83, 88, 95, 117
Athtar 66f, 71, 80, 83, 97f, 103
Athtarat (Ashtoreth) 22, 67, 88

Baal 20f, 30, 36, 66, 89, 95, 106, 109f, 113, 121
Baal (Temple of) 26, 36f, 45, 49, 56, 85, 87–91, 94, 100
Babylon 36f, 86, 102
Barr, J. 109
Bauer, H. 28–30
Bernhardt, K-H. 99
Bethel 113, 116
Bronner, L. 120
bull terminology 83, 113f, 116f
Byblos 37, 48, 53

court 53, 63f
creation 83, 118
Crete/Cretan 18, 38, 56, 59
Cyprus/Cypriot 18f, 27, 39, 42, 46f, 56, 59

Dagan 36, 86, 88, 91, 96
Dagan (Temple of) 26, 36, 49, 56, 91f, 100
Dahood, M. 99, 109, 111f
Daniel 75, 78, 95, 97, 99, 104, 106
death 103, 106, 110–12, 121
decipherment 25, 28–30
Dhorme, E. 28, 30
divination 99
Driver, G. R. 67, 77, 79, 95, 103, 105
Dussaud, R. 18

Ebla 36
Egypt(ian) 19f, 24, 27, 31, 36–47, 59, 61f, 88, 95f, 102
El 66–80, 83, 86, 95–7, 104, 106, 113f, 116–18
El Elyon 117
Elijah 112, 120f
Elisha 120
Emerton, J. A. 114
Engnell, I. 100
Enuma Elish 86, 102
Eusebius of Caesarea 31
Execration Texts 37

fertility 22, 83, 86, 102, 119f
festivals 99–103

Gibson, J. C. L. 67, 79, 99, 103, 105
Gordon, C. H. 95, 105
Gray, J. 83, 97
guilds 64
Guti 35, 37

Hammurabi the Great 36f, 60, 96
Hebrew language 28, 31, 108f
high-priest's house 26–8, 49, 90f, 100
Hittite(s) 27, 36f, 40, 42, 44–7
Hooke, S. H. 100
Hurrian(s) 27, 30f, 37, 40, 42
Hvidberg, F. F. 100
Hyksos 38f

123

124

125

939.44
C979

72530

DATE DUE

MAR 16 '88			
APR 27 '88			
MAY 11 '88			

DEMCO 38-297